HIDDEN
KENT

HIDDEN KENT

Alan Major

With illustrations by Alan Major

COUNTRYSIDE BOOKS
NEWBURY, BERKSHIRE

Front cover photograph of Fairfield parish church by Roy Tricker
Back cover photograph of Reculver church by Bill Meadows

Produced through MRM Associates Ltd, Reading
Typeset by Paragon Typesetters, Clwyd
Printed by J.W. Arrowsmith Ltd., Bristol

To my wife Jean, daughters Stephanie and Caroline,
sons-in-law Andrew Buckworth and Martyn Chatfield,
grand-daughters Claire, Frances, Emily and Lorna
for all their help when required and for just being there
(they can see their names in print, too!)
Also
To my long time friends
Tony Blake and Bill Blake
who, in quite different ways, greatly helped me
at a difficult time in my life

Acknowledgements

➤ It has been stated many times before but remains true nevertheless, that a book such as mine with this content would be almost impossible to write without the generous assistance of numerous other people. I therefore am glad to acknowledge their help and record my sincere thanks to all the following who have contributed to the making of this book.

Janet Adamson, Heritage Officer, Folkestone Library; Helen Allinson, Sittingbourne; Di Bailey, Tunbridge Wells; Ray Baldock, Five Ashes, Mayfield; Mrs R. Barlow, Endowed CE School, Hartlip; Eddie Barton, Canterbury; Tony Blake, Chestfield; Victor Bowden, Kemsing; W.T. Buck, Stockbury; Stephanie Buckworth, Sturry; Janice Button, Newchurch; Noreen Chambers, Hon Secretary, Medway Queen Preservation Society; Caroline Chatfield, Sturry; Derek Chatfield, Ash-by-Sandwich; Mrs Peggy Chowns, Shadoxhurst; Mrs Cloke, Littlestone; J.M. Cordwell, Maidstone Library; David Cousins, Librarian, Local Studies Department, Canterbury City Library; Gerald Cousins, Parish Archivist, Cranbrook; Dartford Borough Council Public Relations Officer; Dover District Council, Tourism and Economic Development Department; East Kent Light Railway Society; Environment Bromley; Basil Fehr, CBE, Dymchurch; Charles Forwood, New Romney; M.K. Frost, Assistant Curator, Dover Museum; Bob Gearing, Dymchurch; Irene Hales, Maidstone; Evelyn B. Hammant, Bromley Green Road, Ruckinge; Joe G. Harman, researcher, Dover; Wallace Harvey, Whitstable; Hythe Public Library, Local History and Reference Section; Kent County Council: Area Bridge Engineer – East Kent, Maidstone; William H. Lapthorne, Broadstairs; Rev J.V. Markham, Elham; Peter Morgan, Dolphin Sailing Barge Museum Trust, Sittingbourne; Victor Nutting, Rainham; Mrs Sylvia Oiller, Dungeness Residents Association; Wing Commander Geoffrey Page, DSO, DFC, Battle of Britain Memorial Trust; Lesley and Sarah Parr-Byrne Tom Thumb Theatre, Margate; John Pearson, Head Teacher, Bredhurst Primary School (for gift of video of the school's May Day celebration); John Revell, Whitstable; L. Robards, Ashford Library; Sir David Salomons Society, Tunbridge Wells; Sarum Hardwood Structures, Winchester; Muriel Searle, Bromley; Mr I. Stephen, Collections Administrator, Royal Mail, Tonbridge; Pauline Stevens, Lower Halstow; L.E. Thompson, Royal Botanic Gardens, Kew; Tonbridge and Malling Bolrough Council Leisure Services; A.G. Turner, Petts Wood, Penny Ward, Ramsgate Library; Sheila Watts, Dymchurch; Bob Williams, Upstreet.

Introduction

So many books about Kent contain the same subjects, their authors having only rehashed the well-known facts. It has been my intention to avoid this, for time spent on research uncovers the 'hidden' history of the county, its places and people.

I have also endeavoured to include, sometimes at length, places which are not or are rarely written about in the county literature. When cities and towns are included I have tried to refer to unknown or lesser known subjects.

If your town or village is not listed herein this does not imply I did not think it has anything worth including. The opposite may be the case; there are some 350 towns and villages in Kent and it was not possible to refer to them all at sufficient length to provide interesting reading. However, I would be interested to learn from Kent people about other unknown or hidden details concerning Kent.

I hope my book will afford you much rewarding reading.

Alan Major

Adisham

➤ In 1767 a 'Mr Reynolds of Addisham, Kent' benefited farmers greatly by introducing the kohlrabi (a kind of cabbage with a fleshy turnip-shaped root) to be grown as a field crop for use as fodder in early spring. Cows ate the leafy tops, and pigs dug out the roots. Kohlrabi, however, had been grown as a cottage garden vegetable by rural folk as early as the 16th century. 'Mr Reynolds' was John Reynolds (1706-1779) who lived at the 15th century Dane Court, Adisham, a member of a renowned Kent farming family who himself was famous nationally as well as locally for his successful new ideas regarding farming methods and crops.

Allhallows-on-Sea

➤ Some people would say this is the Kent seaside resort that never quite made it; others, who like peace and quiet, are glad and prefer it as it is. The parish is bounded by the Thames on the north side and in the east by Yantlet Creek. In the 1930s the river frontage at Avery Farm a mile north of Allhallows village was planned as a holiday area and railway trains took holidaymakers to Allhallows-on-Sea station, built 1932, via Gravesend. The station is now closed but in the caravan park can be found the railway's water tower. It is the camping and caravan holidaymakers who have now revived the resort, catered for by a camping and caravan site, beach huts, and grassland behind the shingle foreshore.

Allhallows means All Saints, the name borne by the small 11th century church on its mound. Near the church a family named Pympe had lived for generations on an estate with a mansion, Allhallows House. It is difficult to appreciate while relaxing in the still remote area today that formerly this was considered so important to the county's defence that the wealthy Pympes with other estate owners thereabouts were sessed (taxed) to supply twelve men at arms with weapons and six hobelers for 'the defence of the seacoast at Yenlade (Yantlet)'. A hobeler was a retainer-soldier, a light horseman who was bound to maintain a hobby, a small horse, for military service. They rode about from place to place at night to get information of the landing of boats, men, etc.

A ship was also moored near the mouth of the Yantlet Creek as a coastguard station. No doubt it also served against smugglers, as the whole area was rife with them, the fishermen-smugglers living in a separate village close to the Allhallows foreshore then called Bell's Hard, now the Slough area of the parish. Part of Avery Farm was formerly The Lobster Inn, where smuggled goods were housed until they could be safely despatched inland.

Allington

➤ Today, with its religious retreat run by the Carmelite Friars in Allington Castle, Allington hardly seems to be the place formerly known as the Gretna Green of Kent, but in the 17th century that is exactly what it was. In the Stuart period the vicar of the parish church had a reputation for being lax over the marriage service and not too insistent on asking the relevant questions. Boats would arrive from Chatham and Rochester with couples who, if they had the fee, were wed. As a small parish it rarely had more than 60 people living there but the total of marriages was amazing. There were twelve marriages in 1648; 18 in 1649, 32 in 1650, 38 in 1651, 29 in 1652, 25 in 1653, but none were entered in the parish register for 1654, 1656, 1657. The reason for this is that an Act introducing the publishing of banns in the market place and the registering of details of marriages put an end to such a large number of mostly illegal unions. Details that were registered of the Allington weddings prior to the Act show the majority of brides and grooms were 'widows' and 'widowers' and came from outside the parish.

Examination of other old Kent parish registers may reveal that similar events took place in other secluded parish churches not completely off the beaten track for transport. In the 19th century St Laurence's church at Allington was rebuilt, only parts of the nefarious original church surviving in the north doorway and the outer arch of the porch-tower.

Ashford

➤ It might be wondered what could possibly be hidden in today's modern market town Ashford, whose development has revitalised it in preparation for a major Channel Tunnel railway station, with expansion plans for Ashford's role as Kent's 21st century boom town. Vehicles rush around the ring road dividing inner town from outer suburb Ashford, while in the town pedestrianisation of former traffic-busy roads and construction of modernistic arcades of shops and businesses give the town an air of newness. Fortunately, the core of old Ashford was wisely retained by the planners. Down a short thoroughfare just off the upper end of the High Street in St George's Square, close to the modernity stands . . . a First World War tank.

Visitors may be puzzled by its presence, but this dates to a period following that war when many towns and cities were given such a tank or artillery, but in following years had these removed for various reasons. During the Second World War many were required as metal for the war effort. Ashford kept theirs. Built in 1916 it is a British Mark IV tank, No. 245, weighing 26 tons and 'female', ie equipped with machine guns rather than the cannons used in 'male' tanks. 'She' has an armament of five machine guns and was presented to the people of Ashford on 1st August 1919 in recognition of their service to the country during the First World War, in particular the purchase of various war loans. After the presentation ceremony, savings certificates were on sale and people who purchased them were allowed to inspect the interior of the tank. It is painted and maintained, graffiti-free, and in 1987 a pyramidal roof was built over it as protection from the elements. It is classed as a listed building.

At 1 Middle Row, in the town centre, a plaque records some of the building's history, indicating that the oldest part is 14th century. It was used as the town gaol for several years, but its private occupiers in the 17th century had the simple patterned pargeting (see *Maidstone*) applied to its white exterior. This was renovated in May 1982, hence that date on it.

In Victoria Park, south of the ring road and the railway line, Ashford has a feature dating from Victorian days when no self-respecting town or city was without one – a magnificent fountain, but what a fountain!

Approached on the north side by steps and a balustrade it is huge in diameter and height, towering over the bystander. Known as the Hubert Fountain it was first shown in the Royal Horticultural Society's Gardens, London, at the 2nd International Exhibition of 1862. Afterwards it was erected at Olantigh Towers, Wye, the latter destroyed by fire in December 1903. In 1910 when rebuilding was taking place the fountain was purchased by George Harper, auctioneer, estate agent and art collector, a man who in his mind's eye could see the fountain as a set piece in Victoria Park. Unfortunately Ashford Council did not feel the same way. Harper anonymously offered to present the fountain to them, subject to the council meeting the cost of dismantling and re-erecting it. The council members visited the fountain, received some estimates for the task from local contractors, then thanked the anonymous donor, but no, they could not accept the free fountain. A fervent lover of Ashford, born in Mersham, Harper felt snubbed but thought about the matter and wrote again to the council saying he would pay the costs that ensued if the council would supply the foundation for the fountain and provide the water supply. A further stipulation was that the fountain should always display every 23rd July, his birthday.

On 24th July 1912, the day after his 71st birthday, the fountain was presented to the town. The Buffs band played, the council members and local populace came to witness but Harper could not be there and it was turned on by a niece, Miss Miles. There was to be a tragic sequel. Harper lived at 6 Elwick Road, Ashford and it was his usual practice to walk to work each morning, sometimes then going for a stroll in the area. On 14th August 1912, three weeks after the fountain was presented, Harper followed this practice but was later seen on the railway line; he committed suicide under a train from Cannon Street.

The French cast iron fountain has standing figures at its summit, representing the continents, Europe, Africa, etc, holding up the top-most circular 'basin'. Below these are seated larger-than-life nubile bare-breasted women and bearded Herculean men holding up several basins while alongside them cherubs blow on conch shells and 'water spirits' leer among much ornate, foliate metalwork. When in use the jet rises above the continents' figures, its water falling on 'their' basin and cascading from this on to the basins held by the nubile women and muscular men. Around their feet water jets from numerous holes into the larger surrounding basin and from this spurts through the mouths of the water spirits into the still larger main basin. It was working and in use to commemorate the 1953 Coronation and was restored for the Silver Jubilee celebration in 1977.

Aylesford

St Peter's is another example of churches in Kent whose nave and chancel are not in line, forming a 'weeping chancel' to commemorate Christ's reclining head at the Crucifixion (see *Cuxton, Keston, Stockbury*).

Half a mile west of the village is Aylesford Priory. It was founded in 1241 by the Carmelites, who were then expelled in 1538 at the time of the Dissolution. Their church was demolished and two ranges of the cloisters converted to a dwelling house. In 1930 this was gutted, but in 1949 the Carmelites decided to return. They commissioned Adrian Gilbert Scott to design a new church and to plan the other buildings and surrounds. The new church was to lie east of the medieval church site, on which the congregation now sits during open air services, in front of which is an arcaded shrine.

In 1954 Our Lady's Building Company was founded to raise the funds to build and restore. Eventually it had 25,000 subscribing members all over the world whose donations helped pay for the restoration. The foundation stone was laid in 1958 and building commenced by the Carmelite brothers helped by professional stone masons and voluntary workers.

The new church was erected using only church stones. Some came from the demolished medieval church, more from Boxley Abbey, near Maidstone, and others from a nearby mansion and barn, both of which had originally been built with stone from the demolished church. Crushed Kentish ragstone was used in the restoration of the cloisters. Several Kent companies and people gave materials; others lent scaffolding, a concrete mixer and a dumper. An anonymous donor paid the wages of the stone masons and also for the roof of the Shrine Church of the Assumption of the Glorious Virgin.

The complete area has now either been restored or rebuilt. Most impressive are the smaller shrines away from the main shrine. These have altars and ceramic work carried out by Adam Kissowski, a Polish monk craftsman who worked here during the 1950s and 1960s, using concentration camp heroes and heroines and Biblical themes as inspiration for his work. He died in 1986 and was interred at The Friars. So it was that out of the old came forth the new to create buildings of beauty.

Barham

➤ St John the Baptist is one of the Kent churches to contain a white ensign flag (there is another at Speldhurst). It was the last one to belong to HMS *Raglan*, sunk in a brief naval engagement with the German light cruiser *Breslau* off the island of Imbros on 20th January 1918, with the loss of three officers and 119 ratings. The flag was given to the church by the ship's Commander, Viscount Broome who lived at Maydeken, a property in the parish.

The members of Barham's Women's Institute in the Second World War were fine examples of the impressive role taken by Britain's Women's Institutes and other civilian women's organisations in aiding the war effort. The Barham WI produced 22,759 lbs (10 tons

3 cwt) of jam. They also bottled about 2,000 lbs of pickles and chutney as well as canning various fruits. They had a pig club and a rabbit club, part of the schemes to rear livestock as a food supply. The branch's wartime efforts were recognised in 1942 with a visit from Mrs Eleanor Roosevelt, wife of the then US President, who was touring Britain.

Barming

➤ In 1930 it was decided by the GPO to paint some post boxes blue for airmail letters only, these being mainly in the towns and cities. By 1936 there were 313 of these airmail boxes, but in 1938 it was thought unnecessary to segregate the mail in this way, so the airmail post boxes were withdrawn. One of them survives, however, outside Barming Post Office, but painted 'postbox red' (see *Pembury, Penshurst*).

Bearsted

➤ In the early 19th century the sand in Bearsted parish had an increased value because it was quarried to obtain 'Bearsted diamonds'. According to an 1834 account these were 'small white crystals found in the sand in this parish, very hard and taking a high polish so they are much sought after'. Apparently they were used as brilliants in semi-precious jewellery, but presumably are not sought now.

The last man hanged in public on nearby Penenden Heath, was interred in Holy Cross churchyard, but there is a doubt as to exactly where. In his *A Saunter Through Kent*, Vol XIV, Sir Charles Igglesden writes 'In the churchyard, by the gate nearest the vicarage, is a board that covers the grave of an unfortunate fellow who was innocent of the crime of which he was found guilty . . . He vowed he was innocent to the end.' A second source states 'the grave of the man hanged at Penenden Heath is marked by a tall cedar tree by the gate into Church Meadow.' A third version claims the man is 'interred by or under a large sequoia tree'.

The man was 19 year old John Dyke, who was seen leaving an area of burning hayricks. He was arrested, charged with incendiarism, found guilty at Maidstone Assizes, condemned and hanged. Later, on his deathbed, another man confessed to the crime. I have

14

checked a transcript of the 19th century Bearsted burials register held in the Canterbury cathedral archives. An entry states 'John Dyke hanged at Penenden Heath, 1830'.

It is probable a tree is growing upon his grave, as the church authorities in the 19th century did not permit the grave of a convicted or executed criminal to be marked by a headstone. Dyke at the time of burial was an assumed criminal, and it was the custom to inter criminals publicly hanged at Penenden Heath in Bearsted churchyard. Possibly there are other now forgotten examples therein.

There is also mystery concerning the identity of the three large, prominent, outward-looking stone figures on the three corners of the church's tower. Edward Hasted in Vol V of his *History and Topographical Survey of Kent*, 1798, stated 'On three corners of the summit of the tower are the figures of three dogs or *bears sejant*, for they are so defaced by great length of time that they can but be guessed at. If they represent the latter they might have been placed there in allusion to the name of the parish; if not these figures might perhaps be the crest of the founder of the church.' This comment indicates that due to weather erosion these figures were later replaced with the three at present in situ, which have been variously claimed as 'animals', 'beasts', 'lions'. It is probable, however, that the suggestion they are in fact the lion of St Mark, with a raised foot, the eagle of St John and the ox of St Luke is correct, the fourth corner having the tower turret.

Beckenham

➤ William Cobbett, perambulating around the county in the early 19th century was later to write in his *Rural Rides*: 'When you get to Beckenham, which is the last parish in Kent, the country begins to assume a cockney-like appearance'. By that I assume he meant a London appearance, with 'the sticking up of shabby-genteel houses' as he called them, 'surrounded with things called gardens in all manner of ridiculous forms'.

On the edge of the old Kent-Surrey boundary stood a farmhouse dating back to 1240 on a 178 acre farm known as Kent House. It was so called either from having been the last house seen when leaving Kent, or the first house seen when coming from Surrey into Kent. It stood near Beckett Walk, another name with a Kent association, and was demolished in the 1950s, but is remembered in the name of the local railway station.

A regular visitor to Beckenham was Samuel Johnson, the literary man, who came to see his timber merchant friend John Cator at Beckenham Place Park to advise him on which books to buy. They certainly weren't financial and investment advice books as Cator himself competently acquired farms and land in the area at considerable speed with an eye to future development, his estate stretching from Shortlands to Sydenham, approximately three miles in area. This land purchase was wise planning because in the 1860s the Cator family were able to build new roads and suburban villas which ended Beckenham's days as a village in Kent. In 1927 the London County Council bought Beckenham Place and grounds as a public park, and since 1929 it has been England's largest public golf course.

A more recent literary inhabitant was Walter de la Mare, poet, novelist, playwright, born in 1873 in Charlton, which was then in Kent. He lived with his family first at 195 Mackenzie Road from 1899 to 1908, then moved to nearby Worbeck Road (this house was subsequently bombed in the Second World War), until, needing a larger house, in 1912 they moved to 14 Thornsett Road, Penge, now Anerley, Kent. Finally in 1925 they moved to Taplow, Bucks. While at Thornsett Road in 1912 de la Mare was awarded the Hawthornden Prize for Literature, and in 1913 wrote the classic *Peacock Pie* there.

At the junction of Southend Road and Brackley Road, Stumps Hill, there is situated a rare pillar box of the brief reigning Edward VIII, made at the Carron Ironworks, Scotland.

Bicknor

It is a strange experience to visit Bicknor church. Lonely it stands by a narrow lane on the uplands of the North Downs, three miles or so south of Sittingbourne, come upon by surprise. Around it are only fruit tree orchards and woodland, with some scattered farms and Bicknor Court away to the east. No wall encloses its churchyard overlooked by huge sycamores, yews and cedar. But this church is virtually unique in Kent. Only one other I know has what Bicknor church has – chalk used in its construction. That so unstable a material should be used is questionable, but the countryside hereabouts sits on chalk so it is easily available, dug from pits in blocks.

Outwardly the church looks Victorian, inwardly it is Norman and other periods. The exterior shows facings of flint, also readily obtainable in the chalk, the large, dominant slate roof at one section descending downwards so it is greater in depth than the height of the nave wall. The south-west tower rises only a few feet above the roof, contains two circular bell-vents and is surmounted by a somewhat squat slate roof. Compared with the large entrance porch near it there is an impression of the tower being out of proportion. In 1861 frost began to penetrate and destabilise the chalk walls. It became essential to build the exterior 'skin' of flints to support and protect the interior from this damage, hence the Victorian architectural deception. The nave's smooth chalk block walls have no memorials; bare simplicity is all around, excepting the marble font that seems much too grand, and not in keeping with its surroundings. One of the few memorials is in the vestry, a tablet of 1676 remembering the wit of Elizabeth Edward, the three year old daughter of a vicar of Bicknor. There is an atmosphere of Bicknor church being in a time warp, a place of quiet contemplation; a church, with no village, considered worth saving by the often reviled Victorian church restorers.

Biddenden

Sometimes it is possible to recognise buildings which were originally inns but later converted to private dwellings. Often the original sign still hangs from the wall, or the iron frame that housed it survives. On the Cranbrook road stands the 17th century former Castleton's Oak inn. The true story behind the sign is that a local carpenter, Ebenezer Castleton, at 70 years old thought it was about time he made his own coffin ready for the fateful day. Near the inn site was an oak tree which Castleton got permission to fell, and from this he cut the boards for the coffin. But as he lived another 30 years it was not needed until he was 100 years old. The inn sign shows white-bearded Castleton wearing a smock seated on the coffin, hence the nickname.

On the garden wall of early 18th century red brick Hendon Hall is one of those 'nosey-parker' structures, a tiled and pyramid roofed brick gazebo (see *Faversham*). Probably from it in 1824 the Hall's owners and their guests watched passers-by going to one of those peculiar feats of rural entertainment that were so commonly performed and popular in the 18th and 19th centuries. Held at Biddenden it was advertised as 'The Greatest Undertaking Ever Performed in England'; the walking of 100 miles in 18 consecutive hours by the celebrated Kentish pedestrian Edward Rayner.

There was a rain shower before the start which made the road 'difficult and heavy' but at one minute before six o'clock on Tuesday evening, 13th April, Rayner started. The first six miles were covered in 59 minutes. At 59 miles Rayner was affected by 'a slight sickness' and he continued labouring under similar distress until the 68th mile, then he recovered and 'kept up a regular steady pace, resting at intervals only for refreshment, until he completed the course, coming in cleverly at full speed as if a mile heat, at 7 minutes before 12 o'clock on Wednesday, 14th April, 1824, with 8 minutes to spare'. He was greeted by tremendous 'hurrahs' from the crowd, a band played and even Biddenden's church bells were rung 'joyfully in celebration'.

Bilsington

In St Peter and St Paul church is a hatchment of a Lord Justice, Lord Luxmoor. In the 17th century it became the fashionable practice that upon the death of a member of a noble family entitled to bear a coat of arms, the latter's arms were painted on a large lozenge-shaped wood board, their hatchment. This was then carried at the funeral of the deceased. Following the funeral the hatchment was hung outside the deceased's former residence for up to a year from date of death, then placed on a wall in the church where the deceased was interred, sometimes hung in the family's chapel, if they had one. The custom is rare today but this example at Bilsington was carried at Lord Luxmoor's funeral in 1945.

Whether the deceased was married or single can be deduced from their hatchment. If the hatchment has an entirely black background and the deceased was a bachelor the arms are single, only those of his family; if a widower, the arms are divided into two, having husband's and wife's coat of arms; if a spinster, the arms are single and lozenge-shaped; if a widow, the arms are divided into two and also lozenge-shaped. If the background is half black and half white it means either it was a hatchment for a married man who died before his wife, the left side being black and right side white, or a married woman who died before her husband, the left side white and right side black.

In the churchyard is a roofed frame on which is suspended a large bell. As it weighs over nine hundredweight, one reason for this could be that being too weighty for the bellcote it was placed on terra-firma. Or it may simply have been that there was not enough room for it in the belfry, which already has two bells. It was cast in 1442 and its Latin inscription translated states 'For many a year the bell of St John shall sound'. It may possibly have come from the former Bilsington Priory, but so hefty a bell indicates it cannot have travelled far to this Romney Marsh edge, and most likely it was cast somewhere closer than the London bell-foundries (see *Borden*). In 1936 a writer stated it was housed 'in a cage'. Curiously, Sir Charles Igglesden visited Bilsington church in 1906 but in his chapter on church and village in *A Saunter Through Kent*, Vol VII, he does not mention this bell in the churchyard which he almost certainly would have done if it had been there.

Birchington

◄ In Quex Park John Powell-Powell, who also built nearby Quex House, erected his useful folly that can be seen from afar and sometimes be heard, too. He was an enthusiastic bell-ringer, but while most of these are content to be in a team to ring the local church's bells he wanted his own 'belfry' to practise his hobby. So he had built his square, stone-dressed, red brick, turreted, spired, pinnacled, windowed bell tower or Waterloo Tower to house his peal of twelve bells. The graceful, curved, white-painted spire was modelled on the similar spire on the tower of St Mary's church, Faversham, and is considered one of the best examples of Regency wrought-iron on a building in Kent. With acclamation from the local newspapers and 'a ringing peal of the bells' the tower was opened to the public in 1819 and still is on the last Sunday of each month, June to September inclusive. Powell-Powell wrote changes for his bells and founded the Quex Park Society of Change Ringers, who also still exist and regularly ring Powell-Powell's bells.

Bishopsbourne

◄ The first Englishman to photograph the moon, invent a prism for illuminating specimens on slides during microscopic examination, develop a chemical means of making photographic paper more sensitive to take an image, among other notable inventions, was not an eminent professional scientist, but the Revd Joseph Bancroft Reade, rector of Bishopsbourne from 1863 until his death there in 1870. He was also the first to microscopically examine the fossil organisms in chalk and photograph them, these illustrations being published in 1838. Unlike many other clergy in the established Church who were horrified in 1859 when Charles Darwin's *Origin of Species* was published, claiming that man's evolution was from apes and throwing doubt on the interpretation of the Scriptures,

Reade, being a scientifically-minded man, went so far as to be one of the scientists and learned men who signed 'The Scientists' Declaration' in 1864. This stated their belief that the discoveries of science and the Bible's teaching were reconcilable. The rectory from which Reade in October 1869 observed a meteor so bright 'it illuminated the whole of Barham Downs and valley with its bright magnesium light', was demolished in 1954. Reade is virtually forgotten today, interred alone, his wife Charlotte (died 1882) being buried at Stone, Bucks. He is close to the north wall of St Mary's church, alongside the path under a large stone slab bearing few details, easily passed by until it is remembered this is his rightful place; it was customary to inter a rector or vicar close to his church if he died during his incumbency.

Borden

➤ According to Helen Allinson in her comprehensively detailed *Borden – The History of a Kentish Parish*, 'In August, 1802, William Wise, churchwarden, paid John Greensted 14/- for carrying the bells to Milton Quay in his cart. The following March Greensted went to fetch the new ones. The Leeds (near Maidstone) ringers came and played the opening rounds or changes a week later . . . ' This is interesting as it indicates Borden was in a fortunate position of being able to cart its bells to the nearest port and then have them transported, possibly by barge, to the Whitechapel foundry in London. So other villages on or within the proximity of the Medway and Thames presumably were able to do the same, thus avoiding the task of hauling them along some of the county's poor roads, even in August, when they were likely to be dry and hard.

In the 17th century, however, Henry and John Wilnar, possibly an Ightham family, cast bells at Borden for some 20 years. John Wilnar died in 1640 and his brother Henry in 1644; both were buried in Borden churchyard. Examples of their bells survive at Bredgar, Ivychurch, Cowden, Addington, Eastry, Challock, and other places.

Helen Allinson states the Wilnars cast their bells at Oad Street 'where in 1959 what is believed to be their casting pit was discovered by Eddie Barton. He was ploughing Boundary Field, which is on Woodgate Farm to the west of Munsgore and north of Woodgate Farmhouse. He came to a slight hollow which made him think of the story he had been told as a boy by a very old man. The story went that the devil in a fit of anger had thrown a bell from the church tower and it had fallen to the earth in Boundary Field, making a hole. As Mr Barton ploughed he found that the soil in the hollow was of a different colour from that of the rest of the field. He found pieces of iron conglomerate which he took to Maidstone Museum. They now have no record of this but the site was recorded at the time by the Ordnance Survey. There was a well nearby which Mr Barton covered or capped, and a bank of pure sand. In the Wilnars' time there would also have been plenty of timber.' (See *Boughton Monchelsea, Stockbury.*)

The Rat and Sparrow Club, Borden, started as early as 1901 and continued until about 1960. In 1915 55 rats' tails, 192 sparrows' heads, 3,864 sparrows' eggs and 240 queen wasps were brought to club meetings by members who were rewarded by committee members, most of them farmers. One penny was the going rate for rats' tails, queen wasps paid for by the dozen. The sparrows that were killed in this way were in fact tree sparrows that by flocking were a serious pest to farmers. Eddie Barton commented in Helen Allinson's *Borden* that every member had to collect at least 100 sparrows' heads over the year to qualify for the free annual dinner.

Boughton Aluph

➤ Being on the 'Pilgrim's Way' All Saints church was visited by those en route to Canterbury. Thought to be unique in its former purpose is its south porch, a meeting place or sort of hostel where those wayfarers and pilgrims, single or in twos and threes, awaited others to arrive so that they could form a larger group of pilgrims or travellers before entering and walking through Challock Forest and the King's Wood. A wise precaution, safety in numbers, as this wooded area was the notorious haunt of robbers. To provide some comfort for the waiting pilgrims the porch was adapted, with the surprising installation of the beautiful fireplace complete with herringbone-tile hearth and backing.

A more modern use of the church, arising from its good acoustics, has been as a recording studio. The late counter-tenor Alfred Deller was one celebrity who recorded there.

Boughton Monchelsea

➤ Bell Wood, in Boughton Monchlesea, might indicate that during its existence it had been owned by someone surnamed Bell. Alternatively (see *Stockbury*) could it be named thus as it was a source of timber for local bell-founding? Two miles or so eastwards is Chart

Sutton, home of Stephen Norton, medieval bell-founder of Norton Court, who was buried in Maidstone. The site of his bell founding is unknown; possibly it was not even in the Maidstone area. In addition, only four miles north-east of Boughton Monchelsea is Broomfield, home of Joseph Hatch, 17th century bell founder who lived at the 15th century Wealden Rose Farm. He died in 1639 and was buried in St Margaret's churchyard, Broomfield. Many of his bells still survive in Kent's belfries.

Brabourne

On the south side of the chancel of St Mary the Virgin church is a rare feature to survive in an English church, a heart shrine. It is square shaped and projects from the pier, possibly for use as a small altar. On its flat top is a slab of Bethersden marble incised with a cross within a circle, which may formerly have contained mosaic. Behind it the reredos is archlike, in Decorated style which dates it between 1280 and 1320. Underneath this is a plain shield. In the back of the heart shrine is a recess or 'feretrum' that would have housed a casket containing a heart, encased in silver or ivory and richly bejewelled. Almost certainly this shrine was prepared here for the heart of John de Baliol, Lord of Galloway, founder of Balliol College, Oxford. One of his sons was John Baliol le Scot elected in 1292 as King of Scotland by Edward I, and another Alexander Baliol, Lord of Chilham Castle. He died in 1269, and after having his heart embalmed his wife Devorgilla carried it everywhere with her, even placing it in her husband's chair at meals. When she died it was buried with her in Dulcecor Abbey which she had founded near Dumfries.

Forty years later the Abbey was sacked in the Scottish Wars but the heart casket was retrieved. The preserved heart found its way to Kent, possibly brought here by John de Baliol's son, John Baliol le Scot, after the latter's defeat by Edward I. He lived at Brabourne, then a royal manor, for a short time before being exiled by Edward, when it is likely he gave the heart into the care of his brothers, Alexander Baliol, Lord of Chilham Castle, and Sir William Baliol le Scot, ancestor of the notable family of Scots at Brabourne. Brabourne was then one of the few English churches attached to a Cluniac monastery, the nearest example of the latter being at nearby Monks Horton; and Alexander, being a Cluniac by religion, had the heart enshrined in Brabourne church. The heart shrine, however, is now empty.

The church also contains something else that is believed to be unique in English churches. The easternmost window in the north wall is a complete example of Norman stained glass, unaltered since the day it was put there in the 12th century. Remarkably it survived in 1774 when the rest of the church's stained glass was sold (see *Petham*).

Brasted

➤ After satisfactorily working for an employer for a lengthy period it is still customary for the retiring person to be given a clock. In the past it was also the practice of kings and others to do this in appreciation of 'services rendered'. Dr John Turton (1735-1806) had been appointed Physician to the Queen's Household in 1771, made Physician-in-Ordinary to Queen Charlotte in 1782 and then became Physician-in-Ordinary to King George III and the Prince of Wales in 1797. During 1784-85 Robert Adam designed and built Brasted Place for Dr Turton, using Tunbridge Wells sandstone ashlar, in Palladian style with Etruscan details. For his new house George III gave Turton the clock that had previously been in a turret of the Horse Guards. King George's 'gift' for 'services rendered' is still in a clock turret at Brasted Place on the service wing of the property.

Bredhurst

➤ It is customary to commemorate St George's Day on 23rd April and May Day on 1st May or a day near to it. At Bredhurst a tradition considerably more than a century old combines both to hold an event early in May that is apparently unique to this village, performed by the children of Bredhurst CE primary school.

In the past the children in front of the May Queen strewed local wild flowers at her feet during the procession, while the children following her sang traditional May songs passed on from generation to generation.

Today the traditional procession firstly makes its way from the school through The Street to a grass field. It is led by a child with a raised banner, followed by a page bearing the May Queen's crown on a cushion. After these walk the May Queen-to-be, the previous year's May Queen, May princesses, maids of honour, ladies in waiting, train bearers, bearers with florally decorated May garland hoops, a king, a queen, prince, princess, St George, the Black Knight, Jack in the Green, not forgetting the Dragon and sundry others, including a bride and groom, dolly, teddy bear, chimney sweep, captain of the guard, red-helmeted archers, peasants; all participants dressed appropriately and topically for the occasion.

On reaching the field the participants process around the field to a platform, whereupon Jack in the Green reads a proclamation regarding the new May Queen. She is then crowned by her predecessor, after which she makes a speech and she and her court again process around the field to show the crowd witnesses this has been done. Again on the platform the May Queen and her retinue are entertained by dancing around the maypole, the children achieving various patterns with the ribbons down the pole's length.

The king and queen, princess and archers, then walk about the field in alarm while the presenter broadcasts the dread news in verse concerning the imminent arrival of the Black Knight. Some 'doves' are released from a basket bearing a message to St George to come immediately. St George soon arrives on a white hobby horse. A few brisk thrusts with his sword disposes of the Black Knight.

The presenter then makes another announcement in verse that an even worse calamity is pending, the Dragon. When this beast appears it is an alarming sight, green and brown with a large head out of which projects a fiery red tongue; a hooped back, long tail and, sometimes glimpsed, eight human feet belonging to the four boys bent inside it. Then follows the Pageant of St George and the Dragon. St George again deals with the foe. Some plunges with his sword despatch the Dragon, which almost gladly lies down on the ground. It soon revives, gets to its feet and walks off, while St George is congratulated by the king and queen and the princess whose hand he has won.

Country dancing next follows performed by the younger children to traditional music, then more maypole dancing by the energetic older girls and boys. The May Queen cuts a large iced cake upon which sits a green dragon also made of icing. Various prizes are awarded to children and parents stroll among usual village fête stalls.

On a warm, dry, sunny May day this event is as close as anyone will get in modern times to witnessing an incident from the days of a rural 'Merrie England'. The enthusiasm of all concerned no doubt will ensure the continuance of this tradition.

Uncle Mack's memorial, Broadstairs seafront

Broadstairs

➤ On the promenade overlooking Viking Bay, among the always floral small seafront gardens, stands a waist-high granite memorial. On its sloping top is a bronze plaque showing a man wearing a mortar-board and playing a banjo. He was known to everyone locally as 'Uncle Mack', not to be confused with the other 'Uncle Mac' of BBC *Children's Hour* fame. The inscription reads 'In Memory of Uncle Mack, J. H. Summerson, who entertained residents of and visitors to Broadstairs for over 50 years, 1895-1948. He brought joy and laughter to young and old.'

A minstrel troupe wearing baggy costumes, mortar boards, led by 'Uncle Godfrey' came to Broadstairs in 1895, to play in the streets and on the promenade. Among them is believed to have been 'Uncle Mack'. He commenced his career in London in 1883 as a child performer with a Victorian entertainer, G.H. MacDermott. As MacDermott was known as 'Big Mack', Summerson inevitably became 'Little Mack'.

Summerson must have enjoyed his years in Broadstairs because in 1900 he arrived with his own minstrel troupe, himself and five other black-faced minstrels, also 'Uncles' – Alex, Alf, Bert, Jim and Reg.

Following this, through the 20s and 30s 'Uncle Mack' and the other 'Uncles', dressed in their white frilled costumes and performing on their stage against the chalk cliff, were a part of the summer season entertainment at Broadstairs.

Their act was to sing old favourite and happy songs accompanied by their own music, created with bone clappers, tambourines, and banjos, to perform humorous sketches, and also talk to and involve the audience. They performed on the sands stage in the morning and afternoon but in the evening on the pier. If the sands were too wet for visitors to sit on the minstrels performed on a platform in one of the seafront streets. After the war 'Uncle Mack' continued performing almost until his death. This much loved man died in 1949 aged 73.

Among the numerous other visitors and residents through the years was John Buchan, Lord Tweedsmuir. In August 1914 Buchan, his wife Susan and daughter Alice reputedly rented St Cuby, at the junction of St Ann's Road and Cliff Promenade, North Foreland. The reason was to recover Alice's health after a serious operation, which it did, but Buchan's own health was also indifferent, and unluckily he had to take to his bed for this reason. According to Susan Tweedsmuir in her book *John Buchan, By His Wife and Friends* (Hodder & Stoughton, 1947) 'To distract his mind from the dull bedroom in our lodgings he started on a book. The Grenfells (relatives by marriage) were also at Broadstairs. They had been lent a villa on the North Foreland: the tenancy carried with it the privilege of a key to what our Nannie called the "private beach", a small cove which was reached by a rickety wooden staircase. How many steps there were I do not know, but John hit on the number thirty-nine as one that would be easily remembered and would catch people's imagination. The staircase to the private beach has now disappeared and has been replaced by an imposing iron or steel erection. When this was done we received a small block of wood in the shape of a step bearing a minute brass plate with the words "The Thirty-Ninth Step".' She adds 'If he [John] had not had to go to bed *The Thirty-Nine Steps* might never have been written.'

What her book throws light on regarding Buchan in Broadstairs is that she several times refers to them being in 'lodgings' but not at St Cuby, whereas her cousin Hilda Grenfell had been lent a villa with a private staircase, which does sound as if it was St Cuby.

Obviously Buchan and Susan would have visited their relatives at St Cuby and seen the staircase. Further details reveal that there were originally 78 steps. St Cuby still overlooks the site of the staircase, now replaced by stone steps which anyone can use.

The work of replacing the unsafe oak staircase was undertaken by a local builder, W.T. May. The owner of St Cuby requested that any of the oak in a sound condition be salvaged for use. The builder's carpenter, Frederick Summers, made three pairs of bookends with it. One was inscribed with a silver plaque bearing 'Made from one of the original 39 steps'. One pair was kept by the owner, a second pair was given to John Buchan and the third pair to Alfred Hitchcock who had directed the first film version of the book in 1935. Some of this film was made at St Cuby using the chauffeur and housemaid. St Cuby is called 'Trafalgar House' in the book, near 'Bradgate', one of the numerous old names for Broadstairs.

At a house he bought called Roselawn, in Kingsgate, Broadstairs, lived another author who created a character as famous in his day as Harry Potter. The author was Frank Richards. He was born Charles Hamilton in 1876 and died on Christmas Eve, 1961. The character was Billy Bunter, and from 1946 to 1961 Richards published thirty-nine Bunter books in addition to thousands of short stories under his twenty pen-names, one of which was Gillingham Jones.

Margate has one of the smallest theatres in Britain; Broadstairs has one of the smallest seaside resort cinemas, the Windsor, which could aptly be called 'The Cinema by the Sands'. It was built in 1911 but to contain an armour museum and known as York Gate Hall after the York Gate, almost adjoining the Hall, across Harbour Street. Its exterior on the sloping street deceives regarding its interior size. There is a tiny foyer and access to the small 29 seat balcony at street level, while downstairs there are 126 seats. The noise from passers-by and vehicles in Harbour Street is deadened by an extra foyer door. There is a once nightly programme of top star films and no breaks for sales or advertisements! It is independently run by R.H. Field, whose cinema is no doubt a welcome venue for holidaymakers, not necessarily always in inclement weather.

In the wall of 41b Callis Court Road, Reading Street, a stone plaque can be seen, placed there to seal a hole made in the wall during the Second World War. This allowed easier passage of fire hoses through the wall to reach a large lake used as a static water tank, in the three acre grounds of Elmwood, the former home of Alfred Harmsworth, Lord Northcliffe. The lake, crossed by a rustic wood bridge, was divided. In one side were goldfish, roach and other ornamental fish;

on the other side, in summer, a Florida alligator that visitors could view and feed from the bridge. Lord Northcliffe's alligator 'pet', however, spent the winter indoors in a warmer conservatory.

Bromley

◣ Unbelievably ironic as it may sound, some of the later rebuilding of London destroyed in the Great Fire of 1666, especially St Paul's cathedral and the London Bridge approaches, was financed by . . . a duty paid on coal coming inside what is now London's Metropolitan Police District! The boundary of the duty area was shown by 'Coal Posts'. When this reconstruction was achieved, however, the duty continued to be levied. Merchants receiving coal inside this boundary area had to pay 4d a ton duty; the coal suppliers rendered returns to the authorities, and City appointed inspectors checked these and the duty payments. As the years passed the sum raised in this way financed various public works; seven Thames and Lea bridges were free of toll payments, Holborn Viaduct was constructed, and assistance given for Thames Embankment work. When the London County Council was established in 1889 the coal duty was no longer levied.

There are 23 Coal Posts in the outer London borough of Bromley. Most existing now, known also as City Posts, were erected by the City of London in 1861, and are sited beside roads, lanes, boundary fences, even on open heathland. They were made of cast iron by Henry Grissell, at the Regents Canal Ironworks, Eagle Wharf Road, Hoxton. They are six ft long, usually three to four ft above ground, the rest below ground, though some examples are buried much deeper. They bear the shield of the City's Arms and an inscription referring to the Act under which they were set up, but those posts with the short inscription '24 VICT' were presumably made before the 1861 Coal and Wine Duties Act was passed and so before its full regnal year and chapter were known. Some of the inscriptions were later covered with correcting plates but these are now broken or lost. The Coal Posts can be recognised because they are painted white, red and black. They are all listed by the Department of the Environment (DOE) and most are maintained by the borough councils.

Two other types are in the Bromley area, both beside railway lines. One erected after 1861 is a cast iron obelisk about five ft high with metal shields originally attached to each of the four sides, sited on private land south-west of the railway near Warren Road. The

Coal Post, Leaves Green, Bromley

second is a tall stone obelisk about 14 ft high, erected before 1861, 500 yards west of Swanley railway station. It bears the City of London Coat of Arms and motto *Domine dirigie nos*. As they had been neglected for many years, in 1985 Bromley Council surveyed the posts, ensured their stability, put upright those that were leaning, cleaned and repainted them. At the completion the Mayor of Bromley on 16th August 1985 unveiled a renovated Coal Post at the junction of Farnborough Hill, Sevenoaks Road and Green Street Green High Street, where an interpretive plaque has been provided. In the London Borough of Bromley 23 Coal Post sites range from near Leaves Green, Downe, Green Street Green, Orpington, Chelsfield to Swanley station. The Environment Bromley offices issue a map. When you have found them all here remember there are over 200 encircling London. Don't forget, too, the 'London Stone' at Upnor.

As for the heart of Bromley it is evident that the arrival of the steam railway in the then market town in 1858 brought about changes, with the High Street being virtually rebuilt. In his *Highways & Byways in Kent* in 1907 Walter Jerrold stated 'In the neighbourhood of Bromley are still pleasant walks . . . and still some fairly rustic lanes, but great are the changes within the past quarter of a century.'

Some buildings are not so old as they may seem. Near the Market

29

Square but in the High Street is the Royal Bell Hotel of 1898, a mix of panels of pargeted strapwork (decoration of interlacing bands and forms similar to fretwork or cut and bent leather), lead-covered bows and 'Tudor' gables, with a very large impressive sign that cannot be missed. Some really old survivals of original Bromley are the red-brick walls of Bromley College at the end of the High Street which have wrought-iron gates of 1666, the Fire of London date. The finials of the stone gate-piers are in the form of bishops' mitres, the Bishops of Rochester having had a palace at Bromley. The college was formerly what we would call today an almshouse. In his will of 1666 the Bishop of Rochester, John Warner, left a sum to build such a property 'for 20 poore widowes (of orthodoxe and loyall clergymen)'. The widows seem to have been kept in some comfort, with two ground floor rooms, two bedrooms and a kitchen. However, each widow had to be attended by one resident servant and a spinster daughter if possible! Even older is the red-brick, half timbered The Old Cottage in Bickley Road built in 1599 on the east side of town. Here it sat behind its brick wall and gateway, also of 1599, while suburban Bromley sprang up around it.

Bromley Green

◣ At the end of the First World War many ex-servicemen on returning home wanted to be their own boss on their own land. They were encouraged in this desire by speculators selling land for market gardens, pig or poultry farming. An example of a poultry farming scheme was at Bromley Green, 1¼ miles east of Shadoxhurst, north of Ruckinge. A woodland had been put on sale by the owners, a London insurance agency, and was bought by a Mr Brake. The woodland was divided by him into plots, on average 200 ft long and 10 ft wide! However, those with enough money could buy as many plots as they required, as many necessary anyway to get sufficient width for a dwelling and other buildings.

Two hundred plots were sold in Bromley Green Road, from Shadoxhurst into Ruckinge parish, adjoining Forty Acres Wood and Bishops Wood; 178 plots in Bromley Green Road adjoining Long Hurst Wood and Chequertree Wood; 67 plots in Main Road, later Ham Street Road, to Ashford, adjoining Forty Acre Wood; 43 plots in Main Road to New Romney, adjoining Capel Wood; 28 plots on Capel Road to Bonnington, adjoining Woodreve Farm and Twelve Acre Wood.

The first requisite was to clear the woodland, no easy task getting roots and stumps out of the clay. As soon as enough room had been opened the would-be poultry farmers either constructed their own wood shacks or bungalows or bought a prefabricated dwelling and erected it. Several purchased ex-army huts while some of the Canadian ex-servicemen used their own timber to build a log cabin. The men could then live on site and clear remaining trees. As time passed the majority gave up and left the area. Few had had enough money or any capital to fall back on when costs, poultry food, etc rose, while prices obtained for eggs and chickens fell. Some failed through lack of experience and knowledge of poultry, their diseases, and so on, while some had the misfortune to purchase bad or unsuitable stock, even when advertised in national poultry publications. Most of them did not realise the cost of failing to fence their land, so they didn't bother, and foxes took a toll. There were also too many poultry farms close together.

When it became necessary to change from free range to battery operation, deep litter, etc most of those still poultry farming finally gave up the struggle. Some remained on their land and got jobs in Ashford or locally. Others sold the land and property and left, being replaced by people who just wanted to live in a rural area but also on some land of their own. They renamed their dwellings Belle Vue, Myrtle Grange, The Haven, Killarney, Clare Lawn, Ashdene, Oakdene, Rosalie, even Mr Jones.

In the Second World War the Army commandeered some of the dwellings and did considerable damage to them. After the war many were demolished as change came to the area, to be replaced by brick properties, not always on the original foundations but on a more suitable site. However, several of the original dwellings, Chesterfield, Hillside, Little Dale, Birchwood, externally and internally improved to modern standards, survive at the moment of writing, but for how long before time's ravages overtakes them cannot be predicted. They stand as a sort of memorial to idealistic men, perhaps too ambitious, some would say foolish or gullible, who through their own endeavours tried to achieve a better life standard for themselves and families, but failed in the attempt.

Brookland

➤ St Augustine's church is renowned for its detached belfry, but for me the attraction of this Romney Marsh church is a much less obvious object and within the church – its hudd. Until the 18th century officiating clergymen and mourners on wet, windy days

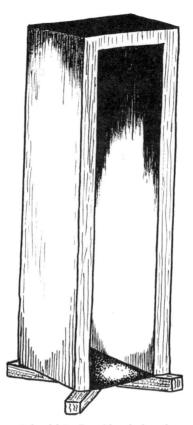

A hudd in Brookland church

endured inclement conditions and got soaked. Then, in that century the graveside shelter, the hudd, or hood as it is sometimes known, was introduced; a tall, man-wide wood structure similar to a sentry box. This was placed alongside the grave on a wet day and within it stood the parson, keeping wig and surplice dry, while the others huddled around in the rain. Eventually it fell into disuse; perhaps later generations of parsons felt they should suffer such inconveniences with their flock.

Also within the church, at the west end of the south aisle, is another curiosity, a wooden enclosure known as a tithe pen. In this the corn, cloth, wine and other contributions due to the parson from his parishioners were weighed out.

Canterbury

➤ Travellers entering or leaving Canterbury West railway station daily pass by a grey plaque. It states: 'Near here was the terminus of the Canterbury & Whitstable Railway, 1830 (George Stephenson, Engineer). The world's first railway season tickets were issued here, 1834.' Several station buildings dating from Canterbury's early involvement with railway development can be seen nearby.

Although Canterbury is visited for its famous attractions it is worth a visitor's effort to see some of the other curious, unusual, and less well known sights that would otherwise be unnoticed.

At the junction of Palace Street and Orange Street above a shop doorway is fixed a replica of a hand water pump painted red. The original pump stood over a well in Palace Street. In 1870 during road works the 'Old Red Pump Well' was rediscovered after having been filled in and the pump removed. Apparently the pump was erected on the nearby premises as a sign and there it remained until it decayed, to be replaced by the more recent replica. It was red presumably so it could easily be seen as a water source in the event of a fire.

Opposite the red pump and still in Palace street is a building with a painted wall sign that proclaims 'Traditionally the Mayflower Inn of the Pilgrim Fathers, 1601', depicting also a sailing ship of the period. The connection between Canterbury, Pilgrim Fathers and the *Mayflower* is that the leader of the expedition, Robert Cushman, a Canterbury grocer, was married in nearby St Alphege church. He obtained the *Mayflower* for the voyage. Another Pilgrim Father was James Chilton, a Canterbury tailor, who sailed with Cushman and it is probably both men, with others, met at the inn, which is now a restaurant.

From King's Bridge, in St Peter's Street, or more clearly from the bridge over the Stour in The Friars, can be seen a tall pointed tower on a small chapel-like building. It is said to have been an alchemist's tower or chimney, although this is unlikely since alchemy flourished from the 13th to the 17th century whereas the tower appears to be no more than 100 years old.

On the 14th century tower of St George's church, all that survives after the church was bombed in 1942, is a large prominent clock projecting over the pavement close to a new shopping development in St George's Street. The clock stopped when the church was hit by bombs. As the tower was unsafe it was decided to demolish it and clear the site. The public, however, protested so the tower was restored and the clock repaired. On 6th May 1955, at 12 noon, the reinstalled clock was unveiled. The clock frame is supported by a crouching stone figure with a pained expression, not surprising as the frame and clock weight 23 cwt. The clock, however, originally had a white face with black numerals and hands; the clock today has a black face with gilt numerals and hands.

In the cathedral's precincts is the Kent War Memorial Garden, formerly the canons' bowling green. The wisteria on top of the garden's west wall is reputed to be the second oldest in England. According to the records at the Royal Botanic Gardens, Kew, the first wisteria was introduced from North America by Mark Catesby in 1724. One of the memorial garden's walls has three niches or ledges, low down and several feet apart, with angled bricks as a 'roof' over each one. These are 'boles' in which stood a bee skep when the medieval monks kept bees. Altogether there are ten bee boles in the walls.

The garden's memorial is to the sons and daughters of Kent who died in war, comprising a Cross of Sacrifice, with a crusader's sword, a ship and a wreath of roses and lilies carved on it. It was unveiled in 1921 when the garden was officially opened. To form part of the Memorial Garden a limestone block was brought from the ruins of the Ypres Cloth Hall, inscribed with the double Cross of Ypres, and set into the city wall's flint bastion facing the memorial cross.

Graffiti is not a new bane on city buildings and the cathedral has not escaped, there being a lot of very old graffiti, mostly initials, names, dates, on the exterior and interior. Unusual are the incisions on the south side of the roofed cloisters where flat stone seating adjoins the full length of the cathedral facing the cloister bays. In the seating are 56 incised shoe patterns or 'sole and heel prints' made by former King's School boys, as in the 18th century the cloisters acted as a playground for the nearby school. The pupils passed the

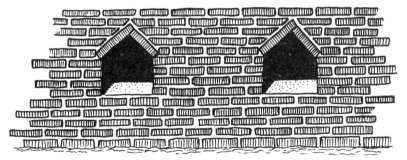

Bee boles in Kent War Memorial Garden, Canterbury cathedral precincts

time by placing a shoe on the stone and with some implement incising around it. Several outlines have initials on the 'heels'. Different is the example where a boy traced around the fingers of a hand. There are also numerous boxlike 'buildings' cut with a flag and flagpole, several of these also with initials of long dead boys.

A memorial of a different type is the 'General Gordon Tree' in Canterbury cemetery, Westgate Court Avenue. After news of his murder reached England a funeral service was held in the cathedral on 13th March 1885. The *Kentish Gazette* reported that 'held at 4 o'clock it was attended by troops from the local Cavalry Depot, Canterbury's Mayor and Councillors and citizens, many of whom were in mourning. In the evening a muffled peal was rung on the cathedral bells and all day flags in the city hung at half-mast'. Curiously the local newspaper made no mention of it but some time during that day a tree was planted in the south-west corner of the old section of Canterbury cemetery. An almost illegible metal plaque at its base states: 'This tree was planted on March 13th, 1885, in Memory of General Gordon who fell at Khartoum, January 26th, 1885, while serving his country.' Who planted the tree is not known. Was it the local council or patriotically-minded citizens who paid the cost, and did the mayor do it on their behalf before attending the cathedral service?

The tree is unusual, being one of the silver lime species of lime trees, getting its name because the leaf undersides are silver and so conspicuous when the wind moves the leaves. Perhaps it was chosen because some of the silver limes are native to China and Gordon may have seen them when serving there. The five-inch leaves are much larger than those of the common limes in Britain. During the 1987 hurricane the 'General Gordon Tree' was badly damaged and branches were torn off or splintered, but through expert tree surgery the remaining five high upright limbs appear healthy.

Capel-le-Ferne

➤ Between Dover and Folkestone, on the clifftop site of a wartime artillery battery position overlooking the English Channel, is the Battle of Britain Memorial. In the late 1980s one of the battle's pilots, Wing-Commander Geoffrey Page, decided to put his long-held idea for such a memorial into being. A Battle of Britain Memorial Trust was established and at first it was planned to create a huge aircraft 'wing' as a memorial. Eventually it was realised this was not practical and instead a figure of a fighter pilot was decided on. The memorial, which cost £250,000, was unveiled by Her Majesty the Queen Mother in July 1993.

Access from the A20 road near the Valiant Sailor inn is direct into a car park. A few yards along a curving, downward sloping path leads the visitor through a gap in the high bank to a large open turfed area surrounded by high grassed banks, except on the Channel side. In the centre of the area is a raised Portland stone base. Seated in the middle of the base reached by steps is the one-and-a-half times life size figure of a young pilot carved in Bixhead Blue sandstone from the Forest of Dean by a Cambridge sculptor, Harry Gray. The pilot is wearing 1940s flying clothes, holding helmet, goggles and gloves, while carved around him in the Portland stone base are the crests of the 66 RAF squadrons that fought in the battle in 1940. The expression of the figure is alert, watchful, ready for the next Luftwaffe raid. Leading to the centre and cut to expose the bare chalk are the long shapes of three propeller blades, so that from the air it can be seen that the pilot sits at the centre of a white three-bladed propellor, an appropriate, fitting memorial to this group of brave men; those who died, those who survived.

There are also remains of other coastal defences – observation posts, radar stations, gun batteries, munition stores, pillboxes, constructed in the area in the 1940s as part of the wartime defences. This can be discovered by following the footpaths along the White Cliffs.

Chalk

Not surprisingly the place takes its name from the chalk and flint soil – in Saxon cealc meaning 'a chalkstone'. According to Hasted, in the past the area was renowned both in England and Europe for the quality of its gun flints, claimed to be higher than those produced in East Anglia. Several flint knappers worked at the craft in the Chalk area. In the 17th, 18th and early 19th century large quantities of gun flints were needed for flintlock firearms in England and they were exported to Europe.

After the flint was dug out of the chalk it was dried, then struck with a hammer to quarter it along its planes of weakness. Using a lighter hammer these quarters were split into smaller flakes, each with a bevel edge along each side like a chisel blade. Then using a special chisel-headed hammer the flakes were reduced again in size to not quite square gun flints. They were made in the appropriate sizes for musket, carbine, horse pistol, large gun, small gun, or pocket pistol.

With the abundance of flint in the chalk in Kent it is to be wondered why the craft seems to have died out in the 18th century and why it did not continue here as long as it did in East Anglia, only ceasing there in recent memory.

On the west porch of St Mary the Virgin's church, above and below an image-niche, is what is described as a 'contorted grotesque' in stone. Its identification is uncertain. Theories have been put forward that it is Puck, whose origin goes back to pagan mythology (see *Smarden, Grain*) or, as it reputedly holds a flagon between its thighs, it has also been associated with brewing church ale.

Chartham

For over 400 years generations of the Terry family were the farriers and blacksmiths at Chartham, until the last, William Terry, with no son to continue, retired in the 1960s and then the forge closed. When discussing family history with me he stated that one of his early ancestors had shod some of the horses of Henry VIII's retinue on its way to the Field of the Cloth of Gold, at Andren, France, a meeting held between Henry and Francis I of France in 1520 to seek an alliance between their two countries. It was so called because of the splendid apparel of the flower of both nations' nobility, their horses and servants. Family legends handed down tend to be 'embroidered' with time and the retelling, but it seems unlikely in this instance, and is supported by facts.

In May, 1520, Henry and his retinue left Greenwich Palace for the meeting. They passed along a route where they would obtain hospitality – Otford Palace, Leeds Castle, Charing Manor House, reputedly Tonford Manor, Thanington, finally arriving at Canterbury on 25th May. So Henry *had* come this way but, it might be thought, the main road bypasses Chartham. It does now, but didn't then. The alteration to today's route came much later, in the 1840s, due to the construction of the railway line through the parish. The road then, via Charing, on reaching Shalmsford Street west of Chartham, turned east over Shalmsford Bridge, climbed the rising ground towards Chartham Down and then at Bolt's Hill turned northwards to Chartham village astride the main route to Canterbury. Henry's retinue comprised 4,334 persons and 1,637 horses. Is it not conceivable that some of these would need shoeing and that conveniently there was a farrier named Terry at Chartham? While awaiting attention the horses could be tethered on the Green or in the meadows by the Stour. In the 1840s the village farrier and blacksmith was George Terry; the village baker was a . . . John Mayger.

Chart Sutton

▀▄ Norton Court, Chart Sutton, was built in the 14th century by Stephen Norton, the Kent bell-founder. Hasted in 1798 referred to it: 'Norton Place is an ancient manor and mansion in this parish though now and for many years since made use of only as a farmhouse. It was originally the property and residence of the family of Norton, to whom it gave name and in the south windows of this church there were formerly effigies of Stephen Norton who lived in King Richard II's reign with his arms: Argent, a chevron between three crescents azure. The partitions inherent to gavelkind so diminished the patrimony of this family that in the reign of Queen Elizabeth I and afterwards they were obliged to sell off several parts of it at different times all of which at length came into the possession of Sir Edward Hales, whose grandson also Edward Hales purchased of the two co-heirs of the Norton family, the seat itself with the remainder of the land belonging to it.'

That event related by Hasted I know to be true as Stephen Norton, through my maternal grandfather, Joseph Norton of Great Chart, is an ancestor of mine, proved by our family tree dating back to 1381 when Stephen Norton died. It was apparently an easy tree to compile because all the son and daughter descendants of the various Norton families stayed in Kent and within fairly close proximity to each other. The majority came down in the world as it were through gavelkind, by which the father's lands were equally divided among all his sons, including illegitimate sons (female descendants were excluded). But some of the Norton 'branches' did well and prospered, one of them marrying into the Knatchbull family in Kent, she being Elizabeth, daughter of Sir John Norton of Faversham.

Stephen Norton was interred in Saxon St Mary's church, Maidstone, which was demolished and rebuilt in 1395, the tomb being lost in what is now All Saints church, Maidstone.

It was in April 1779 that St Michael's church was struck by lightning and set alight; the nave and chancel were destroyed except for the bare walls, and the south windows were also destroyed by the fire's heat. A pity as I would have been interested to see whether Stephen Norton had any family resemblance.

Chatham

➤A traffic-busy link between Chatham and Rochester is that known as New Road, but how 'new' is it? New Road is in fact 200 years old. In the 1760s Rochester's 'citizens' decided to secure an Act of Parliament which, among other developments, would provide for the construction of a road 'to avoid inconvenience of passing through the town', meaning crowded Chatham. Perhaps they also felt trade was moving from Rochester High Street to adjoining Chatham High Street. The outcome was that in 1769 the Act was passed for the road to be financed by tollgates at each end of the New Road. This was in effect an early bypass and, as now, Chatham's unhappy shopkeepers thought trade would pass them by, but it did not. The wide road, built in 1794, was cut parallel to the High Street on high land to the south, overlooking the river Medway and town, from Star Lane in the west, now Star Hill, to the bottom of Chatham Hill in the east. It led also to housing development along the route, on the Chatham side; Gibraltar Place, a three-storeyed, red-brick, 14 house terrace dated 1794 being one example.

In New Road is an obelisk erected by the officers and men of HMS *Barfleur* in memory of the ship's crew members who died taking part in the 1900 Boxer campaign in China. On top of the Great Lines, to the north of the town, for all to see wherever they are in Chatham, is the Naval War Memorial to sailors from Chatham-based ships who were lost at sea in both World Wars. It was designed by Sir Robert Lorimer in 1924 as a counterpart to those similar at Portsmouth and Plymouth.

'The Lines' as it is commonly known is now 90 acres of public Downland leading from behind what was Chatham's Town Hall, opened in 1900, eastwards to Gillingham. The area was designed in 1756 and constructed as a means to prevent a land attack against the dockyard, with ramparts, bastions and ditches. These were added to later with gun batteries connected by tunnels and other defence works. Manoeuvres were held in the open areas attended by royalty, nobility and the public. In the 19th century, about the second week in November, annual horse races were held on the summit of 'The Lines' organised by the county and borough members for Chatham and Rochester. The races lasted two days and were attended by 'all classes of populace'.

In Railway Street, just north of Chatham railway station, is the Waghorn Memorial. Erected in 1888, it is a large statue of Chatham-born Lt. Thomas Waghorn, RN, (1800-1850), pioneer of the overland mail and goods route to India via Egypt. One hand points as if in the direction of his overland route, but unfortunately the wrong way. He should be pointing south with his left hand, not north with his right.

Chiddingstone

➤ One of the several notable families who lived hereabouts were the Streatfeilds in the so-called 'castle'. Thomas Streatfeild (1777-1848) was a topographer and genealogist who planned a great work, *A History of Kent*. He spent years forming a collection of manuscripts, material and specimens and sent out a prospectus about the project but it received little interest from the public. He toiled away but by his death it was still unfinished. The work was bequeathed to his fellow antiquary, Revd Lambert Larking, Hon Secretary of the Kent Archaeological Society, to dispose of as thought fit. The 52 volumes in the collection are now in the British Museum archives. But could this man have given George Eliot (1819-1880) the idea for the character of Casaubon, who never finished his great work in *Middlemarch*?

Thomas Streatfeild is interred in the large Streatfeild sandstone mausoleum in St Mary's churchyard. Unusually, entrance is through a wooden door in a small square 18th century building that looks rather similar to a gazebo. There is a long flight of steps and at the top of them is a terracotta bust of the founder Henry Streatfeild who designed and built the vault in 1736. On either side of the passage way at the bottom are large stone slabs on brickwork and on these lie up to 60 coffins that were all made from wood obtained from trees grown on the Streatfeild estate. The church contains many Streatfeild memorials, but herein are their earthly remains. The coffins are well preserved and this may be due to there being a false altar tomb to the north of the entrance with a grating that allows a current of air to flow through the vault.

Another local family were the Woodgates. It appears during the Civil War, 1642-48, some of them were for Parliament, others for the King. As is the case in these circumstances it split the family apart. A Woodgate commanded a Parliamentary troop of horses. With his men he was not above plundering his locality of Chiddingstone and even robbing his own kinsmen. Forty pounds was taken from Thomas Woodgate, £7.19s.8d from a Walter Woodgate, while a Robert Streatfeild had £22 taken and had to pay

£5 as a ransom to recover two horses seized from him! A William Everest had a horse seized, Thomas Bassett a sword and belt, a Mr Powell a mare. The value of the plundered items was £133.8s.4d. Other fines and forced 'loans' raised the total to several hundred pounds. The parish records carefully listed these details. Perhaps later when the king was restored to the throne they were used in retribution and settling of old scores.

There is a local belief that the plunderers did not get all their own way. A John Woodgate, aged 22, was buried at this time in the church. Between Hoath and Wellers Town in the parish is a cottage called Battle Oak where the fighting is reputed to have occurred.

In the grounds of Chiddingstone 'castle' you can find a 'Penfold'. Postal historians will know that this is the oldest postbox design, a hexagonal shaped pillar box designed by J.W. Penfold in 1866. The Chiddingstone postbox, which is an original, has recently been renovated and is in use during the summer months. Before arriving here it was in regular use at St Pancras goods station, London. There is also a 'Penfold' erected two years ago in The Pantiles, Tunbridge Wells, but it is a replica.

Chilham

In the 18th and early 19th century the vicar was often the only educated man in a village. In addition to caring for his flock, he sometimes taught local children the basic three R's and the scriptures, or he may have been partially assisted in this task, when benefaction funds were available to enable him to pay 'a good woman' to teach a number of boys and girls, the boys to read and write in English and cast accounts, the girls to read English, learn to knit and do plain sewing work.

Originally an early school was held in the north transept of St Mary's church. Then the priest's chamber situated over the south porch was used as a schoolroom in the 18th century, entered by a spiral staircase in the wall. In 1949 repairs to the roof of the chamber made it possible to obtain the large, heavy, long wood table and bench therein to place in the church, immediately on the left-hand side of the nave after entering through the tower. The upper surface of the table, which seats perhaps six pupils a side, maybe more if young children and they squeeze together, is a mass of cut initials, houses with pointed roofs and other incised doodlings, as well as year dates, the earliest being 1753. It has to be wondered how pupils achieved all this if under the eagle eyes of the strict teachers of former days. The bracing struts at either end of the table should be noted, badly worn away, possibly by the boots and shoes of watchful teachers sitting there through the years.

By the organ is a well-preserved four-wheeled Victorian bier that was used to carry the coffined deceased on their last journey to church. It is curious that close to each other within the church is the table at which pupils sat to learn lessons for their start in life and the means that probably carried some of them back to church, life's course run and ended.

The church clock has also moved places in its time. Then only having one hand, it was installed in 1727, at a place lower down the wall in a position that can still be seen. It was taken down and resited 20 ft higher up in 1755, then in 1790 taken down again and replaced with the addition of a minute hand for which the parishioners paid the sum of £6.

In the nave there are four old corbels supporting the roof timbers depicting the winged man – St Matthew, the winged lion – St Mark, the winged ox – St Luke, and the eagle – St John (see *Bearsted*), the symbols used in the Christian Church for these four Evangelists.

On the north side of the tower chamber under the ceiling can be seen two carved wood corbels that are almost 'grotesque' (see *Grain, Smarden*). One is a hairy satyr-like figure with rudimentary horns; the other, slightly more presentable, of a man wearing a crown, both with skinny limbs, reminding me of several examples on buildings in Canterbury's streets. Could these also have been put there to scare away 'evil spirits' around the bells? So far no convincing explanation has been made why these two figures are here.

Chislehurst

➤ In the High Street is the Church of the Annunciation built between 1868 and 1870 of Kentish ragstone, a hard rock, this being left naturally bare both inside and outside the church. This scheme was also used by James Brooks, the architect, for his All Saints church, Perry Street, Northfleet, 1868-1871. Curiously, the tower, to the south-east, is built diagonally to the church.

Opposite the entrance to Camden Place is a property, Cedars, that was formerly the home of William Willett, Jnr (1856-1915), a builder who in 1890 bought Camden Place and developed the estate in two parts for 'commuter houses'. Chislehurst, after the arrival of the railway, had become a fashionable suburb for the homes of London businessmen. If Willett is remembered for anything it is for being a tireless advocate of the Daylight Saving Scheme, to give an extra hour of daylight in summer. Unfortunately, Willett died too soon, as BST was put into effect as a wartime measure in 1916. He is interred in St Nicholas churchyard, Chislehurst.

Therein is also someone who was said in newspaper terminology to be 'able to travel at the speed of light'. Sir Malcolm Campbell (1885-1948), the racing driver and pioneering land and water speed record holder, didn't move quite that fast but in 1935 he held the land speed record at 310 mph and in 1939 the water speed record at 141.7 mph.

Inside St Nicholas church is a monument to Sir Philip Warwick (1609-1683). He became Secretary to the Lord High Treasurer in 1661 because he was 'an incorrupt man who during seven years in the management of the Treasury made but an ordinary fortune out of it'. In his will of 1682 he left £100 of his 'ordinary fortune', the interest of which was to be applied 'to binding to sea service a boy of the parish'. Puzzling as Warwick had been a soldier, not a sailor, serving in Charles I's army as a Volunteer at the Battle of Edgehill.

Another Chislehurst will was that of Revd G. Wilson in 1718 who gave his house and land to pay 20 shillings yearly to a fit person to instruct youth in singing psalms . . .

Across the road from St Nicholas church on the Green is a large circular indent with a smaller interior ring mound. This is the remains of one of the few cockpits surviving, cockfighting being made illegal in 1834.

Cliffe-at-Hoo

➤ It has the only church in Kent dedicated to St Helen, legend stating she was the daughter of Coel, Colchester's 'Old King Cole' of the nursery rhyme. Until a fire in 1520 Cliffe was an important port on the Thames having links with the kingdom of Essex across the river. West of the village are a series of lagoons dating from 1934 created by clay extraction for the area's cement manufacture, cement from works here being used to construct the Eddystone, Needles and Lizard lighthouses.

Astonishingly, after the Second World War Cliffe was suggested as the site for the third London Airport, the Victory Airport. It was intended to combine large passenger-carrying seaplanes using a Cliffe terminal on the Thames, in which no doubt Shorts Brothers, seaplane makers at nearby Rochester, would have been commercially interested. Land passenger-carrying aircraft would have used runways constructed on the north Cliffe marshes. As with the Eynsford scheme it went no further than being a plan.

Cooling

➤ It would seem unnecessary to tell the world why a castle had been constructed, but this John de Cobham did in 1381 when he applied to Richard II to fortify his manor house. The tide used to flow up to the castle then, bringing the risk of attack from the sea, though now there is over two and a half miles between castle and Thames. (A fact realised when in the course of the clearing of 'rubbish' away from the walls of the castle in the 19th century, a 'large vessel was cut through', this apparently being an unidentified wooden ship's hull.) In 1379 the French had sailed up the river and burnt the villages in the vicinity which concentrated the king's mind to grant John de Cobham his licence to build. On completing his castle, outer and inner wards with curtain walls, connected by a drawbridge over a moat, he fixed to the gatehouse a copper tablet that has been restored since and can be seen high up on the east tower. The inscription states:

'Knouwyth that beth and schul be
That I am mad in help of the cuntre
In knowyng of whyche thyng
Thys is chartre and wytnessyng'

Henceforth the manor house was known as Cooling Castle.

The two-towered gatehouse and parts of the curtain wall are all that survive in recognisable form of de Cobham's castle and when visitors see the complete 40 ft high impressive gatehouse topped by battlements they sometimes assume it *is* the castle, but the remains of this are within the gatehouse's entrance across the dried up moat.

A 19th century writer on Cooling and area recorded that a Thomas Murton, a farmer on the Cooling Castle estate, found a use for one part of the castle by annually holding his Harvest Home supper in the castle's former chapel. Here 70 to 80 of his labourers were 'regaled with true olde English hospitality'.

In the graveyard of Cooling's St James the Greater church are the 13 lozenge-shaped chest stones marking the 18th century graves of various Comport children, none of whom lived to be older than 17 months, killed most likely by the area's scourge, malaria. The

Comport family are said to have been organisers of smuggling in the area and to have even hidden some of the smuggled goods inside Cooling church – under the pulpit.

Cranbrook

➤ Sir Charles Igglesden, in his *A Saunter Through Kent*, Vol VII, 1906, refers to a wedding custom at Cranbrook. Formerly, as they left St Dunstan's church, it was customary to strew the path in front of newly-weds with items symbolising the bridegroom's trade or craft. If a shoemaker they had to walk over leather parings; if a blacksmith over scraps of iron; if a carpenter on wood shavings; if a butcher on a sheepskin or two laid on the path; and so on. The custom was almost certainly one performed to ensure employment and good fortune during the marriage, but I have not found it practised elsewhere though it is likely to have been so in villages as a marital folk ritual.

In May 1840 occurred the Great Fire of Cranbrook, which Igglesden also refers to but there is a rather surprising side note to this event in view of the supposed reluctance of the insurance trade to pay on fires and disasters until fully investigated and proved to be an accident. The fire occurred at the High Street premises of James Benzie, an upholsterer, cabinet and chair maker, who had only moved in the previous week. He had not actually insured although he had made plans to do so with John Thomas Dennett, a Cranbrook publisher, bookseller and agent for the Kent Fire Office. The loss incurred by Benzie was in the region of £1,000. It ended on a happier note, however, for according to the *Maidstone Journal & Kent Advertiser* of 2nd June: 'We are happy to learn that the Kent Fire Office have most handsomely presented Mr Benzie with £625, recognising his intention to the agent of his desire to insure, although the insurance was not formally affected'. No doubt this publicity did the insurance office some financial good, too! The building in the High Street is still standing and it is possible to see the change in colouration of some of the bricks on the parapet.

In the church is a memorial plaque to Boyd Alexander (1873-1910), an ornithologist, and to his brother Claud Alexander (1878-1904). His brother accompanied Boyd on his first expedition to cross central Africa from the Niger to the Nile. Claud died at Maifoni, Nigeria; Boyd was killed at Nyeri, Central Africa, by natives. Boyd Alexander's collection of birds of Kent is exhibited in the Cranbrook Museum.

Crockenhill

➤ Even Kentish-born people are confused as to which is which between this place and Crockham Hill. Crockenhill is south-west of Swanley, on the B258; Crockham Hill is south of Westerham on the B2026. The former, from the turn of the century until the 1950s, was the most important area in Kent for growing . . . peppermint. A George Miller at Wested Farm, Crockenhill, planted three fields with the herb. By 1922 Miller was known as 'The Peppermint King', also having land under peppermint cultivation at Warren Road, Chelsfield. In the 1930s, when Albert Miller took over from his father, 420 acres of it were growing, supplying British demand and even exporting it to Europe. The young plants of peppermint, *Mentha x piperita*, were obtained from rooted dark green-leaved plants and planted in fields in the spring. They were kept hoed between the rows and hand weeded to prevent other plants growing among them.

In the late summer when about 20 inches high they came into bloom with spikes of pinkish-mauve flowers and it was then that they were harvested. The parts of commercial use are the leaves and flowers. The stems were usually cut by hand and left in rows. The women didn't care much for the hand cutting as they seemed regularly to get sniffling colds at the same time, they claimed through the peppermint, but this is dubious as peppermint contains menthol, a powerful antiseptic.

The cut rows were called windrows and were lightly lifted up periodically and turned like hay to let air thoroughly dry the stems of flowers and leaves. The stems were then collected into piles and put into open-ended hessian bags and tied. These were loaded on to horse drawn carts and hauled to the farm, then taken by steam-lorry at that time to an old-established Mitcham distillery company, W.J. Bush. Incidentally, Albert Miller was also the last farmer to grow Mitcham lavender at Mitcham for distilling there.

On arriving at Mitcham the peppermint was put into a still which would contain an average of the crop from one to two acres. It was trodden down by the man filling the still, who then sealed the still and passed steam through the peppermint. The resulting liquid was condensed and then drawn off to yield an oil of varying quality. In 1935 Albert Miller had founded Albert Miller (Swanley) Ltd, with his son, Cyril. On his father's death in 1946 Cyril Miller took over and cultivation of peppermint continued, but it was no longer a valuable sideline to the farm's income from fruits, vegetables and corn. It had fallen to only 14 acres grown in 1947 but even this was claimed to be the largest peppermint crop in Britain. In 1958 the last peppermint crop was grown and marketed from Wested Farm, and so ended the cultivation of peppermint on a large scale in Kent. Wested Farm's 18th century farmhouse, the oasthouses and large timber-framed barn survive in use though today cultivation has expanded into different crops. Could the cultivation of peppermint and lavender return? (see *Grove Ferry*). No doubt it all depends on economics.

Crundale

◄ Hereabouts is steep, narrow-laned Downland horse riding country. Appropriately at the entrance to St Mary's churchyard, between the double wooden entrance gates and a small brick mortuary, is a large horse-mounting block. Usually they were made from local stone, ragstone, flints; in other counties granite, sandstone, etc. Occasionally later blocks were made with bricks as this example is. Measuring about three ft high and three ft square the red bricks are surmounted on their top by a single flat stone slab, this being reached by three steps on the churchyard side. The horse was led to stand alongside the laneside edge of the mounting block, the rider ascended the steps and mounted the horse (see *Ightham*). The double gates have carved on the left-hand gate DUM VIVIMUS, and on the right-hand gate VIVAMUS.

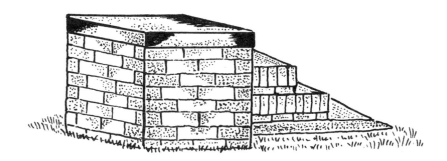

Mounting block and steps, Crundale church

Cudham

➤ The Blacksmith's Arms, Cudham Lane South, Cudham, began in 1638 as a farmhouse with stables. Then a blacksmith set up trade there and it stayed in that craft until 1729 when it was a smithy and beerhouse. In 1730 a sign was erected showing it was entirely an inn and so, with Victorian extensions, it has remained.

One of the landlords was Richard Relph, who may never have been recorded by history if one of his 15 children had not been Harry, born at the Blacksmith's Arms in Cudham. Later the world was to know Harry as 'Little Tich', the music-hall entertainer as he was only four ft tall. Aged twelve he made his first stage appearance at the Rosherville Gardens, Gravesend. Later he was to appear not only in London and throughout Britain, with such stars as Dan Leno and Marie Lloyd, but also in New York and with the *Folies Bergère* in Paris.

He had soon realised his own name was a bit too mundane, so he thought about a stage name. In the 1870s there was a famous impersonation case known as the Tichborne Claimant trial. A Wapping butcher's son, Arthur Orton, had arrived in Australia claiming that he was the lost at sea Roger Tichborne, heir to a Hampshire estate. Orton, a man of large girth, a 'big Tichborne', got 14 years gaol, and Harry Relph got a stage name, 'Little Tich'.

He was always immensely popular in his varied sketches, plays and pantomimes, the audiences relating to 'Little Tich' as the 'eternal little man being done down', but perhaps his greatest stroke of brilliance was when he decided to use a pair of long-toed shoes in a comedy cum acrobatic dancing act. He became rich but never forgot his early days when he whistled outside London theatres for halfpennies and slept on the Embankment, and for years afterwards he revisited his birthplace. His last appearance was in 1927 with Jack Hylton and his band at the London Alhambra. He died in 1928.

In the Blacksmith's Arms a pair of his original shoes, 28 inches long, with other stage props he used, are housed in a glass case.

Cuxton

➤ Other churches in Kent also have an eccentric ground plan, deliberate or accidental (see *Keston, Stockbury, Aylesford*), but that of St Michael church, Cuxton, on its Medway hillside, has passed into

Kentish folklore. Usually churches are basically on an east-west axis; Cuxton, formerly Cookstone, or Cuckstone, has a south-west axis. The nave and chancel are Norman, with much 15th century work and 19th century additions and restoration. The north porch and some of the buttresses have been realistically described by one writer, John Newman in *West Kent and the Weald*: 'stone spotted with flint like currant pudding'.

There are several slight variations to the old Kent jingle: 'If you would goe to a church mis-went, You must goe to Cuckstone in Kent'; 'He that would see a church mis-went, Let him crawl to Cuxton in Kent'; 'If you would see a church mis-went, Then you must go to Cuxton in Kent'. A saying with wider English use was 'Very unusual in proportion, as Cuckstone church in Kent'. The saying may have originated with Dr Robert Plot, the antiquarian at Borden in Kent in the 17th century, in a letter he wrote to a Bishop Fell referring to 'If you would goe, etc'. William Hazlitt in his *English Proverbs*, which refers to numerous Kent sayings, quotes another source 'So said because the church is very unusual in proportion', Hazlitt adding 'It refers to Cuxton near Rochester'.

Dartford

➤ Queen Elizabeth I was graciously pleased to grant a licence on 17th February 1589 to John Spilman, her jeweller, goldsmith and papermaker, giving him the monopoly to make white writing paper. He established the first successful commercial paper mill in England near Powder Mill Lane, Dartford. The later Spilman family's finances declined and in 1732 their paper mill was sold to become a gunpowder factory, but by then, through them, paper making was an established North Kent industry.

Far from successful was an earlier enterprise Elizabeth was involved in. The Earl of Warwick had financed Sir Martin Frobisher, the navigator, for a private expedition to find the North-West Passage from the Atlantic to the Pacific Ocean. On going ashore on an island during the expedition one of Frobisher's seamen picked up a lump of black rock and took it back to England as a souvenir. He showed it to an Italian chemist named Agnello in London who said the rock was gold bearing. Other goldsmiths said it was worthless, but such was the quest for gold at that time, when the Spanish and Portuguese had the monopoly of countries containing it, that if an island existed they did not know about which the English could seize, it had to be done. Queen Elizabeth I, usually a shrewd woman, was confident when she loaned some of her warships to Frobisher to sail to the same region, with instructions not to bother about the North-West Passage but to find as much gold bearing rock as possible. When his ships returned they were carrying 200 tons of the black rock. Some of it was locked in Bristol Castle, some in the Tower of London, but tests on samples did not seem so encouraging regarding its precious content. So Frobisher went back to the Arctic and returned with a further cargo of 1,200 tons of the rock to London docks. The first tests in the Tower Hill furnaces were supposedly 'successful'.

So in 1577 a column of packhorses loaded with the black rock and guarded by heavily armed men arrived at Dartford Priory. Here efforts were made to refine the black rock and get the gold. As the firings proceeded, however, it was soon realised this was not to be. A mere, in our money, forty pounds worth of minerals was recovered from 26 hundredweight of the black rock. Not enough to pay the cost of the expeditions and the ships' crews. Refining work stopped and the heaps of useless rock were abandoned. The black, coarse-grained rock was peridotite, a dark rock composed almost entirely of the minerals olivine and pyroxene.

The event is little known but there is evidence from this fruitless venture that can still be seen today because later the black rock was used to repair the Tudor Priory boundary wall, a length surviving in Kingsfield Terrace.

British towns and cities are often 'twinned' with overseas counterparts, but an industrialised town like Dartford seems hardly the place to be 'twinned' with the Royal Air Force, which it is. The origin of this goes back to the First World War when an aerodrome existed at Joyce Green, which Royal Flying Corps pilots used for training. It was not ideal for this and there were crashes. It was often waterlogged and pilots did not find it encouraging to be surrounded by high chimney stacks, an explosives factory and a hospital. Vickers Ltd also carried out gun testing in the area. In the Second World War Dartford raised £500,000, equalling 100 Spitfires, to buy aircraft through the 'Wings For Victory' campaign. No. 32 Squadron had been formed on 12th January 1916, and used Joyce Green aerodrome, which was involved in the pioneering trials on the development of radar for early warning and fighter control. During the Second World War it played a role in the Battle of France and in the Battle of Britain, becoming the RAF's top scoring squadron. In recognition of the long standing links between Dartford and the Royal Air Force, the affiliation 'twinning' the town and No. 32 Squadron was signed on 14th November 1990.

50

Deal

◢ On Dover's seafront is a statue to C.S. Rolls, who in 1910 was the first Englishman to fly an aircraft from England across to France and back on the same day. There is also a bust of Captain Matthew Webb, the first man to swim the English Channel, in 1875. Deal could possibly erect its own statue on the long seafront to . . . William Jarman. His feat was equally one needing courage and strength and was achieved without any prior preparation. He simply rowed across the Channel to France! On a Friday morning in December 1911, 19 year old Jarman decided to row from Deal to France by means of an 18 ft skiff, accompanied by an Italian in another skiff. Soon after setting off the weather became hazy and the Italian decided to turn back. Jarman continued alone, without food or water and only a compass to set his course. About halfway across he was sighted by a passing yacht and with the camaraderie among seafarers on this perilous element the crew invited Jarman aboard for a meal, which he readily accepted. Then he set off again for France, finally reaching the French shore on the Saturday afternoon of the next day. He hauled the skiff up into some sand dunes and not surprisingly lay down and slept soundly. It is not recorded how he returned, whether he rowed back again or used the conventional means. Perhaps he was not the first to row the English Channel and as he was not officially making the attempt, he has not gone into the record books, but this young lad's feat is all the more remarkable as he had to cross or row past some of the most treacherous water in the world, including the Goodwin Sands. Unlike the others he has been forgotten and unmarked by history, although the *Kentish Gazette*, on 17th December 1911, thought his achievement worth some of its space.

Another Deal inhabitant, however, has been remembered in stone but for a tragic reason. Some 2½ miles north of Deal, between the resort and the Sandwich Bay Estate Hotel, on a path west of the Royal Cinque Ports Golf Course stands Mary Bax's Stone, a small memorial erected in the grassy bank. A sad event caused it to be placed here. On 25th August 1782 Mary Bax of Deal was walking along this path or hereabouts when she met a man dressed in seaman's clothes. He demanded the parcel she was carrying and when she refused to hand it over the man murdered her and ran off with it. But the foul deed had been witnessed by the son of a 'looker', a sort of marsh shepherd who cared for sheep and cattle, ensuring that they did not fall into dykes, etc. The boy gave the alarm and the murderer's description. The latter was captured in Folkestone churchyard, Martin Lash, a Swedish seaman who had deserted his ship lying off Deal. Lash was tried and hanged at Maidstone. The public erected the stone to the victim's memory, but now only the words 'Mary Bax, Spinster' are legible.

Killing in defence was arranged for at Deal's castle, approached only from the west, off Victoria Road. The original iron-studded main oak door is reached along an abutment across the deep moat and then over a short modern bridge on the site of the drawbridge. When standing here look up and you will see five vertical holes in the roof of the passage way. If you were an unwelcome caller trying to force entry at the door when the castle was part of England's coastal defences the holes would probably have been the last thing you would have seen. From them would be discharged on you boiling oil and quicklime (not molten lead, difficult to manipulate, very expensive and too useful to the defenders to use in this way), or a mixture of missiles. For this reason they are called 'murder holes'.

Dover

➤Today Dover is thought of as the main English port for Europe, or vice-versa, where visitors arrive or depart, a place only to pass through. The Victorians and Edwardians knew differently. They thought of Dover not only as a port, but also as a resort, to sit on the beach, watch the ships arrive at and depart from the harbour and, yes, see the steam engines hauling goods wagons along the seafront to the harbours and piers. When visitors tired of this they strolled to the Connaught Gardens in the shadow of the Castle or climbed the grassed Heights. After many years in the doldrums this belief in it as a resort is returning, fostered by the district council. An attractive step has been taken with the pedestrianisation of Market Square in the middle of which is the centre-piece, a fountain. This is a Bell Arm Fountain, specially designed for Dover by Uistigate Ltd of Gravesend. The cost, including plumbing, the pool and water feature, was £30,000, money well spent as it has become a focal point for visitors to the square.

Alongside it is a water feature of the past, a very large granite animal drinking fountain and trough, filled with flowers, bearing the Biblical quotation 'Blessed are the merciful for they shall obtain mercy'. This trough had an uncertain start as to where it was going to be sited. In 1884 a Mr and Mrs Johnson sold a café in Snargate

Street, and being charitably minded offered £100 from its sale to provide Dover with such a trough and fountain (see *Pembury*). The first suggested site was just beyond Buckland Bridge, to be near the Gate Inn. Then it was alternatively suggested to be somewhere on the town side of Dover Priory station, then near the Old Crabble Toll Gate, followed by yet another suggestion of it to be sited 'near the Museum'. A different councillor proposed a site below a terrace at Buckland, but this was vetoed by another who said it should go outside the Prince Albert inn. The councillors' suggestions moved it to and fro in Dover until it was finally unanimously agreed that the site should be near the Elms Junction. The council's surveyor promised to have it in position in a week, no doubt keeping his fingers crossed that the councillors would not change their minds again. It is not recorded what Mr and Mrs Johnson thought of all this shilly-shallying over their gift. There it stood on Elmsvale Corner until removed from the site to stand in the Connaught Park nursery before being brought to the refurbished Market Square about 1989.

Little known to visitors is Connaught Park, reached from the Market Square along Castle Street to Castle Hill Road, left into Connaught Road, then to the Castle Gate entrance or Lodge Gate entrance. There had been no need for a park all the while it was possible for people to wander on the Western Heights and open ground close to the town, but when the Heights were fortified and the building development of the town increased a demand arose about 1881 for a recreation ground. Voluntary subscriptions by the townspeople raised £2,700 for terracing, lawn laying and tree planting, the Department of Woods and Forests, on behalf of the Crown, agreeing to lease the land to the Corporation for 99 years. About 25 acres of land was taken in hand, from the Lodge entrance up to the gate opposite Godwyne Road. When completed the chairman of the subscription committee, a Dr Astley, handed the keys over to the mayor on 1st May 1883, but it was not formally opened until the task was done by the Duke and Duchess of Connaught on 14th July 1883, the Duchess planting a tree near the park lake. The opening of the park by the royal couple had not originally been intended but as they had a long standing commitment to open the Connaught Hall, the new addition to the Maison Dieu (Town Hall), someone had the idea of getting them also to open the new park which they agreed to do. Shortly afterwards the park area was extended to 30 acres by taking over the whole of the hillside up to the Deal road. The lawned area is in three stages – the Lodge, Centre, and Castle Lawns. There is the customary large goldfish pool, but what comes as a surprise is the bird aviary. Exhibited are zebra finches, budgerigars, and other colourful birds, their plumage and twittering an attraction to children.

Despite its military and naval history, the subject of Dover's war memorial is not akin to these. Sited in Biggin Street, outside the public library, it depicts a life-sized bronze figure of Youth, feet encircled by thorns and hands upstretched to grasp a fiery cross. It was designed by a Dover man, Reginald R. Goulden, and unveiled on 5th November 1924, by a Kent man, Vice-Admiral Sir Roger Keyes, leader of the raid on Zeebrugge, as a tribute to the Dover people who died in the First World War. A plaque has since been added in memory of Dovorians killed in the Second World War. Sir Roger Keyes was interred in St James' cemetery, Dover, in January, 1946, among the men who were killed in the Zeebrugge raid on St George's Day 1918.

In Strond Street stood the Royal Ship and Family Hotel overlooking the Custom House Quay and said to be 'the best known hotel in Europe, and here have reposed most of the crowned heads of the world, ambassadors, warriors, statesmen and poets. Many of the effusions of Byron, Foote and Churchill were written on the panes of the windows. Here Churchill passed his last days and found a final resting place in a humble grave in an old churchyard a short distance from the hotel,' so said a gazetteer in 1847. This was, of course, another Mr Churchill, also famous in his time, Charles Churchill (1731-1764), poet and satirist. He came to live in Dover and was interred in the old graveyard of St Martins church, near York Street, Dover, his grave being visited by Lord Byron. When the new bypass road into Dover was built postwar, a Churchill grave was discovered in the redevelopment there, but the site is now covered with tarmac.

Dungeness

➤Writing in his article *The Little Kingdom of Dungeness* (*Kent County Journal*, Winter, 1935) C.K. Lewis noted 'I daresay it will be hard to believe there is a place in Kent where wild goats are to be found, yet such is a fact. They are not very wild, perhaps, but they are free and unfettered, secure their own living and are a hardy race. These goats have their home in a stretch of Kent which until recent years was almost isolated and at present is not very well known. Nature has played its part in making this district of Kent lonely if not quite inaccessible . . . I started by mentioning the goats. Their origin is remote; they are apparently a mixture of many breeds and in some way are producing a breed of their own because the introduction of well known strains among them has been unsuccessful. Newcomers cannot stand the hard life of Dungeness. These "wild" goats are not so wild, it should be said, that they cannot be milked by the scattered fisher folk; they sometimes go up near the cottages for shelter and are eager recipients of titbits of food. There are 70 or 80 goats altogether. Some are quite tame and will eat out of the hand and those who give milk get a little special care in the shape of food and shelter. At one time, before the advent of roads the goats were the main supply of milk for the residents and it is still the custom to keep a box outside the cottage door for the convenience of milking any of the nannies. In very bad weather they will shelter by the sides of the cottages but for most of the time they live a carefree life in the open spaces, browsing on the scanty herbage and on the shoots of gorse, alder and broom. The bees of Dungeness and their honey have also secured local fame. The wife of the lighthouse keeper, who has an apiary, rarely fails to take prizes in exhibition for the outstanding quality of her honey. Where it may be asked in this rather bleak region do the bees find flowers? Flowers are perhaps not always apparent to the eye of the casual visitor, but they exist nonetheless – thrift, sea campion, broom, furze, yellow horned poppy, sea holly, borage, viper's bugloss, the flowers of the blackberry and the dewberry . . . The holidaymaker has not yet conquered it and in that fact may be found one of its attractions . . .'

Mrs Sylvia Oiller of the Dungeness Residents Association told me the goats were in fact owned mainly by the local fishing community and almost every household owned them, hence the local name for the area, 'Nanny Goat Island'. Another local resident, Mrs Cloke of Littlestone, who has lived in the area since 1930, confirmed the goats were never truly wild in that sense, each goat having an owner, although they used to roam wherever there was food. At the end of the day most would return home of their own accord, but sometimes they tried to stay away. Then a member of the household had to search the area and bring back their goat/s. Rounding them up was often a considerably difficult task, catching and taking them home where they were housed in a 'goathouse', sometimes made of corrugated iron or whatever was at hand. As Mrs Cloke's grandmother kept goats for their milk they existed in the area at least back to the 1890s.

During the Second World War the number of goats declined owing to the expanses of minefields in the area, a hazard for wandering goats unless tethered! At the end of the war, even though cows' milk was available, several families still had goats, one family as recently as 1991.

No longer do the postmen wear 'backstays', pieces of flat wood strapped to the soles of their boots, so they can walk 25 miles or so a day over the shingle delivering letters in the area; vans have eliminated that task. Similarly the wide-wheeled carts that could transport across the shingle have also become obsolete. Visiting the Dungeness area today, with its nuclear electric power station, modern unmanned lighthouse, network of roads with expanses of modern dwellings it is difficult to realise that less than 50 years ago Dungeness was still a world hidden away from the rest of Kent (see *Dymchurch*).

Dunton Green

◄━ Like Hoo, Pluckley, Rainham, Pembury, High Brooms and Newington-by-Sittingbourne, Dunton Green had a brickworks that produced high quality bricks, using the local gault clay, also tiles and pottery. In Knole House archives is a reference to new tiles for it being obtained from a source at Dunton Green in the 17th century. Bricks were also being made in the 19th century in the Kingswood Road and Pounsley areas of Dunton Green. In 1862 the Dunton Green Brick, Tile and Pottery Works was established, with clayholes or pits, kilns, engine house at Rye Lane, offices and brickyard at Pounsley. There were also 16 workmen's cottages and later, in 1935, the large house Pounsley was built, their own Dunton Green bricks being used in their construction.

The company had the first mechanical brick making machine in England (believed French or German), which they imported from the Continent,but it was destroyed when the brickworks was bombed in the Second World War. Several clayholes were worked: these had to be continually pumped when the clay was not being dug out so that water did not collect. When the clayholes were worked out they soon became flooded, the last being used in 1956. One was large in area and 40 ft deep; another smaller clayhole by the 1930s had become a pond with aquatic and plant life, and as the pond had been stocked at some time by the Ministry of Agriculture and Fisheries there was good fishing. Shortly after the end of the Second World War it was filled with rubble from the London bomb sites.

During the hand digging of the clay many fossils were discovered, particularly ammonites (shelled sea molluscs from the Jurassic and Cretaceous periods) and some are exhibited in Maidstone Museum.

The pottery produced not only flower pots, seed pans, bulb bowls, but also chimney pots, chick feeding pans, rhubarb pots, orchid pots, rustic garden ornament 'tree stumps' and bread crocks. Other artefacts were produced, such as tiles with a hole so that they could be hung on a wall, bearing bas relief cricketing scenes. Other artefacts known to be made included dog and eagle models, and one red earthenware wall plaque depicted a coiled snake, another reptile, and four other creatures including a moth or butterfly, probably made for amusement or a special order.

In 1890 St John's church was built with bricks from the works. There is an incredible but true account connected with the clay works and the church. When the church was planned an employee of the works designed the two roof finials that depict a cross within a circle. The design was approved and it was decided at the works to make three instead of two, a spare in case one was broken or damaged during the church building. Forty years later the church was struck by lightning during a violent thunderstorm and the finial at the roof's west end was destroyed. The vicar went to the works to ask if it was possible to duplicate the destroyed finial. The works director said he thought they still had the original spare finial in its straw-lined box in a store. Both went to the store but to their amazement the lightning had also struck the store on the same evening, making a hole in the roof; the box was burnt and the finial smashed. Incredibly lightning had destroyed the spare finial in the store on the same evening that the church had been struck.

Dymchurch

➤ This coastal resort, within the sound and smell of the sea, has never had a main line railway station though there is the station for the miniature Romney, Hythe and Dymchurch Railway, so it comes as a surprise to discover the number of ex-railway carriages sited and in use in the area. Their origins date from the early years of the century until the 1930s. It appears that just prior to or just after the First World War a Canadian had a number of the carriages delivered to the main line New Romney railway station, but what his intention was is unknown. He got into financial difficulties so the carriages were offered for sale, though it was unclear if the railway company or the Canadian then owned them. However, some of them were sold and taken to Dungeness and 16 of them are still there, owned privately, and used for fishermen's huts and holiday homes.

A builder in Dymchurch, Mr Edwin Wraight, decided to buy the remainder, but not for the carriages' structure, his grandson, Bob Gearing of Dymchurch, told me. The seats were stripped out of the carriages for their horsehair stuffing which Mr Wraight needed as a binding constituent in plasterwork. This was presumably done at New Romney. Though Dymchurch was then a small village, Mr Wraight had a substantial business with a large work force of plumbers, carpenters, joiners, painters, etc, also a blacksmith's forge employed in shoeing horses, putting the iron rims on wheels, etc. As he was also the local undertaker he made the coffins required.

After the seats were removed the carriages were resold, the wheels also removed and then transported to the site of the purchaser. The eastern side of Romney Marsh was beginning to be developed as a holiday area but it was still largely an uninhabited plain of shingle and marsh, with pockets of population (see *Dungeness*), lonely though not inaccessible. Ideal for those who wanted to 'get away from it all'.

I understand that later it was possible to buy a carriage direct from a railway company or their agent who delivered it to the site where required. Some were in fact purchased by railway employees, to put on a site they had bought and to live in on retirement. One railway company even established some of the carriages on sites for their employees, mostly from Ashford, to stay in on 'busmen's holidays'.

Prices varied according to condition, from £5 for a basic, usually seatless, carriage, up to £25 or more for one with its fittings, racks, hand washbasin, toilet, etc.

Today at 103 High Street two combined carriages with a roof are effectively in use as the business premises of Ron Ayres, an upholsterer. Before this ownership they were used as an antique shop.

Many of these carriages have been converted into comfortable living accommodation. Some are much altered, others original or nearly so, with leather belts to raise windows and so on. Those which were originally retirement homes or holiday boltholes have since become permanent homes and in the same family for many years, modern generations obtaining a fascination from living in a railway carriage or two.

At Slodden Farm, the home of Mr and Mrs Basil Fehr, is a combination of one railway carriage and wooden house, with the latter built on the side of the carriage. The wooden house, called Slodden Farm Bungalow, in Hythe Road, was built in 1896 when the London Underground changed from wood to metal carriages; the interior was in very good condition and so remained virtually unaltered.

The home of Mrs Sheila Watts, Marine Avenue, Dymchurch, is built of two railway carriages, bought from the LBSC Railway. One carriage is believed to be about 100 years old, the other about 120 years old. The house was constructed using these in 1918 by a previous owner who lived in it until 1963, after which it remained empty until purchased by Mrs Watts in 1979. Other examples are one in Pear Tree Lane; another, Our Den on Tower Estate; and again in the garden of Barn House, Sea Wall Road. This is owned by Dr Coxon a local GP, and was formerly owned by the famous Sterndale Bennett family.

Some of the carriages even returned to being used on a railway. Three carriages which were used for the storage of goods in Wraights Hythe Road builders' yard were later bought by the Kent and East Sussex Steam Railway, Tenterden, rebuilt where renovation was necessary and are now in general use on the route of that railway.

Eastbridge

The only remaining evidence that hereabouts was another of the 'lost communities' of the Marsh is a large part of the west wall of the tower and upward jutting fragments of the ruined church, sited alongside the Dymchurch to Bonnington road near Eastbridge House. The village had a population of 21 in the 1801 census. Other instances of such communities are Orgarswick, Hope All Saints, Midley, Blackmanstone, Falconhurst and Shorne.

Eastchurch

After visiting Eastchurch in 1847 a gazetteer compiler reported: 'The scarcity of fresh water in Eastchurch makes the inhabitants very careful to preserve such falls from the clouds for which purpose there are a number of spouts leading from the leads of the church into large tubs around it in the churchyard. These having lids with locks are sinecures for those who have been at the expense of building them' – a sinecure being the taking of an emolument without work or performance of any duty. No doubt this water complemented that available from wells and would have made commonsense to save. This is the only place in Kent where I have read a record of this taking place, although on consideration it is to be wondered why other parishes did not use the practice. Many churches do now have a downpipe or two direct from the church roof gutter to a water butt; this water is used for plants or vases on graves if there is not a piped water supply. Ironically, Eastchurch on the high ground of the Isle of Sheppey looks down on southern marsh water courses such as The Dray, Capel Fleet, Bells Creek, just as it did when the compiler came this way in the 19th century.

East Peckham

St Michael's church has a mounting block for those who arrived by horse (see *Crundale, Ightham*). Even more grandly it has a timber-framed stable, too, near the lychgate with stalls in which the horses were stabled while their owners were attending the long church services. Still surviving above the stalls are the boards with names of the local gentry. As the village is three miles from its original medieval church it is not hard to realise why those who could afford to do so rode to worship, the less fortunate having to walk.

The church also has an enormous 15th century ragstone south porch (see *Chilham, Hythe, Hawkhurst*). In it is much wall graffiti, claimed to be the work of unruly schoolboys when it was a schoolroom or, more surprisingly, the doodlings of canoodling courting couples, even brides and grooms awaiting the arrival of the vicar to commence the first part of their marriage service in the porch.

Eastry

This was another Kent village that had a rat and sparrow club, whose aim was to keep down numbers of these creatures, classed as 'vermin'. In March 1913 at the Bull inn, members produced 630 rats and 973 sparrows. In January 1933, at a meeting held at the Five Bells inn, 100 rats' tails and 145 sparrows' heads were produced by members. In 1919 the government had introduced a Rats and Mice Destruction Bill and on 29th December that year began a National Rat Week when the public was urged to kill as many rats and mice as possible. Local councils formed rat destruction committees who in turn helped start village rat clubs. However, rat and sparrow clubs were in existence earlier (see *Borden, Upchurch*), paying their members a sum for each sparrow's head and rat's tail. Some of these clubs also killed queen and other wasps.

Edenbridge

➤ About four miles south of where the 'astonishing scene' occurred in Westerham parish in 1596, and four miles south-west of the 1756 Toys Hill 'land incident' five months before the latter, another 'strange phenomenon' took place in this neighbouring parish, Edenbridge. On 1st November 1755 there was a 'surprising agitation' of the water of a pond, an acre in area, divided by a post and rail fence which was almost submerged. On hearing a noise as if something had fallen in the water several passers-by ran to the pond. They were surprised to see the water open in the centre so they could see the bottom of the fence posts, while at the same time the water rushed up and over a bank and then when perpendicular fell back into the pond. The witnesses felt no earth tremor to explain this on the calm, windless day.

However, on 24th January 1758, at about 2 o'clock in the morning, houses in the parish shook strongly enough for furniture and chinaware therein to vibrate. The cause was thought to be a 'minor earthquake' and though people were alarmed no damage to property was caused. But could some of the Edenbridge and Westerham 'phenomena' have been connected?

Elham

➤ In the rural Kentish dialect a 'palm tree' was a yew tree. At Easter, if the traditional 'sallow-willow', 'pussy willow' or 'palm willow' was not locally available, country folk gathered branches of the other 'palm' – yew – to adorn their church and homes. When an inn was so-named in centuries past such a sign would depict a yew tree, even if the inn was called the Palm Tree. One example is the Yew Tree at Westbere (which see) known in 1834 as the Palm Tree. In her *Companion Into Kent*, published in 1934, Dorothy Gardiner confirms 'The "Palm Tree" of sundry Kent inns, one in the Elham Valley, is the homely yew'.

The Elham Valley public house, the Palm Tree at Wingmore, is one of those known to have been a meeting place in the 19th century of George Ransley ('Captain Batts', deported to Tasmania in 1827) and his Aldington gang of smugglers. The sign now depicts a coconut palm tree, but this is almost certainly due to modern artistic licence, or a genuine mistake.

Near to the path and adjoining the south side of St Mary the Virgin church tower is an example of the headstones that puzzle by having an inscription which would appear to state the deceased died in two different years! This says 'Here lieth the Body of Mary, wife of James Irland of this parish, who left issue two Daughters, Elizabeth and Sarah. She departed this life March ye 15th, 173⅔.'

In the church chancel a square Decorated two light window contains a curious example of amateur stained glass. The subject is David, the Minstrel, playing the harp to King Saul when he 'had the evil spirit' (1 Sam. XVI 23). It was designed, painted and fired at the vicarage by Frank Wodehouse, brother of Rev Walker Wodehouse, the then Vicar (1846-1899). What is unusual is that Wodehouse used as models the faces of celebrities at that time. Saul has the face of Thomas Carlyle while David has the face of Madame Adelina Patti, the opera singer! The two figures behind the throne are Gladstone and Disraeli while in the background as Samuel, the High Priest, is the three-times Prime Minister, the Marquess of Salisbury. The figures below are local characters represented by members of the Wodehouse family, with young members of the Royal Family, three of Queen Victoria's daughters. Above are the Arms of the Wodehouse family.

Elmsted

➤ In the rural areas of Kent small Primitive Methodist or Wesleyan brick chapels are frequently to be found alongside a lane or road, built on a remote site on the parish boundary, sometimes a considerable distance from a village. The reason was two-fold – the local Anglican clergymen and squire gentry wanted the Nonconformists to be distanced as far as possible out of their sight when they were worshipping; secondly the Nonconformists equally wanted to be out of sight to worship in their own fashion.

An example of such a religious building is on the Elmsted-Hastingleigh boundary among the deep Downland valleys with their wooded or grassed slopes, but this one, near Evington Lodge, is so hidden from the Hastingleigh-Elmsted road it is easily passed without being seen. It was known as 'the cathedral in the woods' before some of the trees were felled. Now a public footpath past it proves this to be an accurate description.

Its origin lies in the religious dissent of the early 19th century and an expansion of Baptist churches in Kent. In the 1860s the Baptists held open-air meetings on Elmsted village green as the church was 'a very dark place with only one parish church service and no

The 'Cathedral in the woods', Elmsted

Sunday school for children, the latter with parents spending the Sabbath in the village alehouse'. These meetings were surprisingly well attended with new adherents continually joining, so the Baptists decided to raise funds and build their own chapel. In 1869 on payment of £7 10 shillings, ten perches of land were bought from a William Smith at Evington Leeze in Elmsted parish 'on which land to erect a Meeting House to be used as a Place of Public Religious Worship by the Society of Protestant Dissenters called Particular or Calvinistic Baptists'.

Money was raised, materials given and those who had neither gave their labour so that the Meeting House was completed in 1870 at a cost of £90. Every conceivable difficulty had been placed in their way. The employers of the labourers had tried to get the men to stop the work. Some were intimidated in their own cottages, warned to have nothing to do with the construction, but it continued. Those men with vehicles and horses carried materials free and in other ways those who intended to worship there helped by using their craftsmen skills. Even after completion persecution continued, instigated almost certainly by the incumbents of Elmsted and Hastingleigh churches who saw their own congregations declining. One founder was William Marchant, a tenant farmer of nearby Bodsom Green Farm, father of Bessie Marchant (see *Petham*) who was forced to leave the farm by his landlord, Sir Courtney Honywood (buried with many of his ancestors in St James the Great church, Elmsted) and move to Petham. However, the small Elmsted Meeting House, or Elmsted Baptist Mission Chapel as it is now called, was a success, so rewarding the religious zeal and sacrifices that were made to bring such buildings into being. The charming little Mission Chapel is still used for services. A new roof replaced the old several years ago. But because of its isolation and modern morality 'the cathedral in the woods' has to be kept locked when not in use.

On the Elmsted to Petham road one of the hidden water curiosities of Kent, the 'nailbournes' – intermittent streams – rises on land at aptly named Little Bucket Farm, coursing northwards, adjoining the road for some distance before disappearing underground. Then further northwards along the same road it rises again near Duckpit Farm and runs parallel to the road. Then near Petham it moves eastwards along a specially made ditch across a large field until arriving in Marble Pond (the name corrupted from Mardel, surname of a previous owner) opposite Petham's village hall. Thence it makes it way across another field northwards to run behind Petham's Primitive Methodist Chapel in Watery Lane and if the water volume is sufficient bypasses Swarling Manor at the foot of the Chartham Downs to empty itself eventually into the Stour near Shalmsford Street. Worshippers at the Petham Chapel in Victorian times were 'afeared for their lives' when the seeminly alive 'woe water', as they called it, flowed past the Chapel door.

Eynsford

➤ On the wall of a dwelling next to the 1826 Baptist Chapel a blue plaque states it was the home of the composer Peter Warlock, the pseudonym of Philip Heseltine, 1894-1930. Warlock composed over 100 songs, many with a rural theme, his best known composition being his popular *Capriol Suite*. He published a book on his friend, fellow composer Frederick Delius in 1923 and worked with Sir Thomas Beecham to promote Delius' work, Warlock spending four years at Eynsford in the 1920s. He was found dead from gas poisoning in his London flat indicating suicide, though the inquest returned an open verdict.

Eynsford's picture-postcard village attracted many well-known residents. Arthur Mee (1875-1943), editor of *The Children's Newspaper*, prolific author, and compiler of the county survey *The King's England* series, lived at Eynsford Hill. Leslie Hore-Belisha (1893-1957) lived here for a time, though he died at Sholden. While Minister of Transport (1934-1937) he gave his name to the 'Belisha beacon' street crossings and inaugurated driving tests for motorists.

Another resident was Elliott Downs Till, who founded Arbor Day here, Eynsford being the first village in England to follow the American practice of setting aside one day a year to plant trees. Now we have Tree Planting Week.

Till was responsible for several Arbor Days, the first of which, in 1897, commemorated Queen Victoria's Diamond Jubilee. Then trees were planted so the initial letters of the trees' names when put together formed words and phrases. There were four sets. From the railway station (near which there is a VR postbox) to the village on the left-hand side was spelt out a quotation from Robert Browning's *Rabbi Ben Ezra*: 'Grow old along with me, The best is yet to be'. The same opening lines Till had put on an oak frame surrounding the new dial of St Martin's church tower clock when the clock had been removed for repair in 1903. In the meadow on the left-hand side of the village towards the mill from Little Mote Gate more trees were planted in 1901, the year of Victoria's death, spelling one of Tennyson's lines: 'She wrought her people everlasting good'. Around the school other trees formed 'My son be wise' and four trees around what is now the war memorial formed 'Love' – Lime for L, Olive for O, Veronica for V and Elm for E. A few Arbor trees still exist. The village hall was also built at Till's expense and in 1904 Till, a teetotaller, bought the Harrow Inn, renaming it the Castle Hotel. He also altered the premises so the bar and tap rooms were separate from the part used as a hotel. Casual drinking was restricted to the rear of the premises. His instructions to landlords were also eccentric. No ale, beer or other refreshment was to be served on a Sunday, except to hotel guests. Only one alcoholic drink was to be served to each person *per day*! The brewery freeholders understandably were not happy about this as they wanted to increase sales. They took Till to the High Court. Incredibly Till won the case. The brewers took it to the Court of Appeal. They won, Till lost. So ended his campaign, one man, one drink. He died as a result of a bee sting in 1917, aged 82; the lychgate was his memorial, his grave is by the path halfway up the churchyard.

The area would have lost its residential attraction if another form of building had been implemented. In the mid 1930s it was announced Eynsford was to be the site of the new airport for London. Obviously it didn't happen. If it had there would have been a curious parallel with the past because Eynsford was the area where Percy Pilcher, the 33 year old English aeronautical pioneer on the verge of being the first man to fly a powered aircraft, built his Hawk gliders in a shed near Lower Austin and Upper Austin farms, and glided at Magpie Bottom. Unfortunately near Rugby he crashed on 30th September 1899 and died two days later, the first Briton to be killed in a gliding accident.

Farningham

The church guide for St Peter and St Paul church, Farningham, written by Revd Donald Campbell in 1973, gives a brief glimpse of the wartime parish. I quote a relevant paragraph: 'It has been estimated that during the Second World War Farningham received 143 high explosive bombs, twelve incendiary attacks, six flying bombs, one long range rocket and other assorted missiles. By September 1940 air raid warnings had become so frequent that the then vicar, Revd F. Wiltshire, decided to make sure of the church collections by having them at the beginning of the service instead of at the end. Nevertheless Farningham casualties were surprisingly light, about a dozen people being slightly injured and no one killed. There was, however, a certain amount of damage to property. As far as the church was concerned a few stones and tiles were dislodged and a number of stained glass windows were destroyed. In the opinion of some of the congregation the loss of these windows was an improvement. There was now more light!'

It is indeed fortunate that the large stained glass window above the choir stalls was not among the destroyed windows. This is the work of Charles Winston, son of a former vicar of Farningham, who became an expert on stained glass and glass painting and who first revived interest in medieval stained glass in 19th century England. The 10th edition of the *Encyclopedia Britannica* 1902 stated 'Charles Winston, whose *Hints on Glass Painting* was the first real contribution towards the understanding of Gothic glass and who succeeded in getting glass very like old in texture and colour, was more learned in ancient instances than appreciative of modern design.'

One of the windows at Farningham, that already mentioned, is an early example of his work, created in 1832, when he was about 18 years old. It has the family arms of Dr Van Mildert, vicar of Farningham 1807-1815, who later became Bishop of Durham, and the Arms of the Winston family.

Also in the nave there is a small window by Charles Winston behind the pulpit of an archbishop in a 15th century style, based on a drawing by Winston of Simon de Mepham at that time in the east window of Meopham church.

The west window was one of those destroyed. Its replacement in 1954 is interesting because it was the first church window in Britain to portray Queen Elizabeth II in stained glass.

The village hall has a weather vane depicting Wadard, a knight who invaded with William the Conqueror in 1066 and settled locally.

Sparepenny Lane was thus named because of the toll bar at the Eynsford end. Presumably if anyone tried to spare a penny and avoid paying they ended up in the cottages situated on the village side of the A20 roundabout, which sometime in their existence acted as the local gaol.

Faversham

As Faversham is a centuries-old important town and port, first recorded in AD 811 and later as 'The King's Port', a title bestowed for ship service rendered, it's perhaps puzzling today that this Cinque Port was not originally founded nearer the London-Canterbury road (Watling Street). The reason is that when its site was chosen, on ground high enough above the risk of tidal flooding, Canterbury and this road had less *local* significance, whereas the Creek was access to the Swale and vital sea route by which commodities were imported and exported, so the town's trade prospered.

To create a link for easier access from this road and to lure its passing travellers to tarry awhile in Faversham's shops, inns and market, The Mall thoroughfare was constructed in 1773. A few yards from The Mall's junction with Canterbury Road is a wooden gazebo, in the garden of private premises but easily seen as it is higher than the boundary wall it adjoins. These curious wood or brick hut or small house-like buildings with windows and sometimes a tiled roof, were used by the house-owners and their guests for the partaking of tea or other refreshment. There they could sit, dry in the gazebo, and as a pastime gaze at people and vehicles moving past on the thoroughfare below them. An earlier version of peeping from behind curtained windows!

Faversham's market is the oldest in Kent, existing for at least 900 years. It is still held on Tuesdays, Fridays and Saturdays alongside the Regency Guildhall, in Market Place, the central hub of the town. Along the streets and roads leading off it there is visible evidence of the civic pride felt for this attractive town with 400 listed buildings in a multiplicity of architectural styles.

On nearby red-brick 76 Preston Street, next to The Hole in the

Wall inn, a plaque states 'This house was the residence of Edward Jacob, FSA, the Faversham historian (Mayor 1749, 54, 65, 75). His descendants were the makers of India'. Jacob (1710-1788) was a notable early botanist, author of *Plantae Favershamienses, a catalogue of the more perfect plants growing spontaneously about Faversham*. He alphabetically listed 144 new plant records for Kent and used John Ray's system of cataloguing and naming plants. Jacob, a doctor in practice in the town, was also Kent's first palaeo-botanist, cataloguing in his book fossils of plants found on Sheppey.

In Court Street the offices of a world famous brewer are housed in a large building with an ornate front and a doorcase dated 1869. At both ends of the building and on each side of the doorway are larger than life, high plasterwork bines of green hops climbing up straight brown hop poles as they formerly did in Kent's hop gardens.

Next door the plain, white-fronted property also bears a plaque – 'This house was the residence of Thomas Southouse, 1671, Mayor and Author of *Monasticium Favershamienses* (A Survey of Faversham Monastery). James II was brought here from 12 Market Place in December 1688, and stayed here until taken to London. Subsequently this house was residence of Richard Marsh who founded this brewery in 1698.'

As Kent hops and beer brewing have been interlinked for centuries it is appropriate Faversham celebrates with a Hop Festival early in September, with events concerning hops, and bines of hops being sold from stalls. In Faversham's streets numerous local and regional folk groups dance to and play traditional music, there being much jollity and, in the inns and taverns, a-tasting of the brews. Shops are adorned with hop themes and the brewery is open for guided tours.

Abbey Street, which led to the abbey founded by King Stephen and now hidden under a school playing field, is not all that it appears. Behind some of the fine Georgian façades are hidden 15th and 16th century timber-framed residences.

It was at No. 83 that 'Ivorex' plaques, figures and other items were produced by Arthur Osborne. Osborne is something of a mystery figure. His family came from Faversham but emigrated to Massachusetts in the 19th century where young Arthur worked as a tile designer. For an unknown reason Osborne returned to Faversham and at the turn of the 20th century started his business firstly in East Street, then moving to the Abbey Street premises. He apparently discouraged visitors and this caused 'an air of mystery in the town about the secret process he used at the works'. However, his products were popular and by the end of the 1920s he was employing 50 people. His 'process' was to make the drawing of the original design in clay or plasticine, take gelatine moulds, and cast the plaques in plaster of Paris. He then shaded and painted the plaque, figure, etc, in watercolours, finally covering it with a wax seal. Osborne died in 1952. His daughter Blanche continued the business for several years but it closed in 1965. Over 450 different wall plaques, busts and other items were produced and are now collectors' items. The museum in the Fleur de Lys Heritage Centre, Faversham, has specimens. Now we know that the reason Osborne discouraged visitors was simply to protect the method he used to make 'Ivorex' from being stolen by rivals.

In 1965 the site of the Abbey's Royal Chapel was excavated and two vaults exposed in which King Stephen and his wife Matilda had been interred. The Royal Chapel was a mausoleum seven ft by seven ft that would have contained the coffins and their bodies but no trace of either was found. Probably the vaults were unharmed until the dissolution of the monasteries in 1538, after which they were robbed. Thomas Southouse recorded 'when for the gain of the lead wherein this King's body was incoffined his sacred remains were dislodged and thrown into the neighbouring river'. In the Trinity chapel of St Mary of Charity church a brass plate above a stone tomb states 'In Memory of Stephen, King of England buried at Faversham'. Local tradition says the bones of Stephen and Matilda were rescued from the 'river', presumably the Creek, and re-interred herein. The excavation has not disproved Southouse's statement, nor the local belief. Your guess is as good as mine.

Evidence that the Market Place was not always a safe place to be is the true story of Michael Greenwood. While a schoolboy he was walking there one morning in 1748 when he was seized by a naval press gang. In twelve years 'service' he witnessed the execution of Admiral Byng and went on an expedition to the Barbary coast, Africa, during which his ship was wrecked in 1758. Survivors were seized by Moors and kept as slaves for 17 months, until in 1760 the Government ransomed them. Greenwood returned to Faversham and died in 1812 but before doing so wrote his own epitaph on his headstone in St Mary's churchyard where he ended up almost within sight of where his adventures began.

Folkestone

➤Between Folkestone Central railway station and Shorncliffe Road is the resort's Kingsnorth Gardens behind a boundary hedge and virtually hidden from the view of passers-by. The reason for this is that the site originally was a pit of brick-earth which was used for brick making. After being exhausted for this purpose it became a nursery ground, then allotments. It was offered to Folkestone Corporation by William, 7th Earl of Radnor, after whom the nearby park and cricket ground was named. The Corporation decided to create a sunken ornamental garden in formal Italian style on the site. Work commenced in December 1926. It was opened by Lady Radnor in June, 1928. The name, Kingsnorth Gardens, had originally been given to a buildings development started nearby in 1886 so the two were combined. John Kingsnorth (1811-1875) had been a tenant farmer in the area. Sloping paths lead down into the hollow to fishponds, topiary examples, rose beds, patio; and seating allows visitors to sit in the restful retreat warmly basking, while enjoying the banks of flowers, shrubs and trees surrounding them. Wisely the parks department has named these so the public can identify what they are looking at.

Near The Leas bandstand, built 1895, linking The Leas on top with the Undercliff or West Cliff and Lower Sandgate Road below, is the Zig-Zag Path. Prior to this was a steep path up and down the cliff with many steps, too much for the elderly and those with prams and pushchairs. As Folkestone expanded from middle-class genteel clientele to the rail and charabanc visitor it was decided something apposite for all was needed. Following the First World War the answer was a series of low, 1:16, gradient paths, zig-zagging east to west to east to west and so on down the cliff, with level paths at the bends, provided with seats so those who wanted could rest and enjoy the Channel views. A London company, Pulham, specialists in rockwork, were employed for the task. They had developed a type of artificial 'rock', Pulhamite, based on waste material being pulverised in a destructor then mixed with cement. In 1894 they had created the rockwork of the gardens on the approach road to East Cliff, Ramsgate, also the Mappin Terrace at London Zoo in 1910. Firstly they strengthened the Undercliff and filled in the pockets in the natural cliff, sometimes with soil and planted trees. Then the up to 8 ft wide gentle gradient, stepless pathway was built, the sides protected and embellished using Pulham's artificial 'rock'. Some parts of the pathway have rockwork arches and shelters with seats. Opened in 1921 the Zig-Zag Path was immediately popular. A survey in September 1921 discovered on that day 2,630 persons, 37 prams had used the path downwards, while 2,324 persons, 19 prams, and one bicycle had made the climb up the path. In 1970 there were several earth slips causing some collapse of the path. Repairs were done but where this had happened steps replaced the pathway. Protests were made that this removed the uniqueness of the Zig-Zag Path, but to no avail though true. Visitors continue to stagger up it, though of course it is much less energetic to saunter down it, at the same time admiring the similarity of Pulham's artificial 'rock' to the real thing.

The bay windows above the shop premises at 34 Sandgate Road, Folkestone's main shopping thoroughfare, look ordinary but behind them no ordinary person lived. It was the home of Catherine Crowe, Victorian writer on the supernatural. It was even claimed that, because she used scientific research of the day as a basis for fiction, her books were superior to those of her predecessor, Mary Shelley, creator of *Frankenstein*. She was born as Catherine Stevens in London in 1790, but her parents wanted her to avoid the city's temptations, so bought and moved to Borough Green Farm, now Borough Green House, Borough Green, since 1905. Her childhood here influenced two of her early novels, *Linny Lockwood*, in which Borough Green is referred to, and the three-volume *The Adventures of Susan Hopley* which has a Kentish background. When 25, however, she was living in London, then in 1822 married a Lt.-Col. John Crowe. When her marriage ended she wrote children's novels, translated foreign books and wrote 'domestic interior' novels for women. In 1840 she became interested in phrenology, physiology, mesmerism, the supernatural and what we now call psychology. Numerous books followed until her psychic analysis of ghost appearances, *The Night Side of Nature or Ghosts and Ghost Seers*, was published in 1848. At that time there was an upsurge of interest in spiritualism. Two well-known believers were the sisters of Alfred, Lord Tennyson, Emilia Jesse and Mary Ker, living at Margate. So a tract she wrote, *Spiritualism and the age we live in* was nationally popular, but shortly afterwards she supposedly suffered a period of 'violent insanity'. This is untrue and was a story spread by Charles Dickens who vehemently opposed spiritualism. She did have what we would describe as a nervous breakdown in 1854 and recovered, but afterwards wrote no more supernatural and similar works, only children's books in the 1860s. Her only child, Capt. John William Crowe and his family were living in Folkestone, where he was a JP so in 1870, at the age of 80, Catherine Crowe moved into 34

Sandgate Road. There she died aged 82 of 'natural decay' on 14th June 1872. She is interred under a heavy, stark slab, devoid of any display of sentiment or sense of loss, in Cheriton Road cemetery, Folkestone.

Fordcombe

➤ On the outskirts of Fordcombe there is a lane called Beggars Heaven, possibly where paupers were buried or the burial site of plague victims (see *Hougham*). An adjoining lane has a field that is still called 'Dead Man's Field', possibly indicating a former use.

In St Peter's church is interred Sir Henry Hardinge of South Park, Penshurst (which see). He was the second for the Duke of Wellington when the Duke fought a duel with Lord Winchelsea. While sketching at Ligny near the Prussian positions during the Battle of Quatre Bras in 1815 a bursting shell flung a rock so violently it smashed his left hand. As this had to be immediately amputated he missed the Battle of Waterloo.

He was appointed Governor-General of India, where he started the Indian railway system. After his return in 1848 he laid the foundation stone of St Peter's church and paid for most of the construction costs.

Fordwich

➤ Marden has some stocks in its churchyard; Fordwich has its stocks now in the Press Yard outside the Court Hall, which is sometimes also known as the Town Hall, claimed to be 'the smallest Town Hall in England'. The stocks formerly stood by the bridge over the Stour and were moved to the present site for safety and to be close to the other items of punishment. The Press Yard is where criminals from the gaol were exercised and this is where they sometimes also met their end. The name Press Yard came from the Yard or Court of the same name in old Newgate Prison in which the torture of *peine forte et dure* was carried out. In this a felon who refused to answer the charge against him was tortured by having heavy weights placed on him, which were increased until he ended his silence and answered the charge one way or the other. If he still refused he was silenced forever, being pressed to death (see *Hothfield*). Later the Press Yard was the place from which capitally convicted prisoners started for the place of execution.

Stocks in Press Yard, Fordwich

Lenham has its lock-up gaol as a separate building in the village; Fordwich has a gaol as part of the Court Hall on the ground floor, entered by a small exterior door. At the rear of the Court Hall is the Crane House on a bank of the river Stour, both banks of which are the sites of the former port's wharves whereon was unloaded the stone, timber, wine, and other goods for Canterbury, whose port Fordwich was. On the Crane House is a crane to which in the past would have been attached the ducking stool. This was more like a chair, in which criminals, scandal-mongering scolds and argumentative women were lowered into the river as a punishment. Rather thoughtfully, however, on the upper floor in the Court Hall the authorities provided a small room in which the dunked people could remove their clothes and dry themselves. A ducking stool is now kept in the Court Hall.

Anyone found guilty at the Bar by the magistrate on this upper floor and sentenced to imprisonment only had to be taken downstairs to the ground floor to the tiny gaol that held several prisoners in discomfort. The last recorded 'occupants' were three local poachers in 1885, though the gaol was busier in earlier centuries for those guilty of what we would consider 'minor' offences. It is also reputed that a certain well in the area known as 'Thefeswell' was used to execute thieves who, with hands and knees tied together, were thrown down it to drown. This is difficult to believe. A source of water was so precious and protected it seems doubtful our sensible forebears would pollute the water source with criminals' corpses. Hang them on the gallows at the Stodmarsh road junction, yes; drown them by well, unlikely. Why not just toss them straight into the river to float away, then the parish would not even have the cost of burial?

Gillingham

It stands on the wide promenade of Watling Street, between First Avenue and Woodlands Road, overlooking the Medway Estuary; thousands pass by every day in vehicles en route to and from Chatham or elsewhere but to most people it may be just a rather grand clock tower. It is in fact a memorial clock to William Adams, the first Englishman credited with living in Japan and also with being the founder of the Japanese navy. He was born in Gillingham in 1564, somewhere within the vicinity of St Mary Magdalene church, Gillingham Green, and at the age of twelve was baptised at this church on 24th September 1567. He was apprenticed to a shipmaster, Nicholas Diggins of Limehouse, afterwards serving on coasters and merchant ships, becoming a master and pilot in Queen Elizabeth's navy and for the Worshipful Company of Barbary Merchants.

In 1598 he was appointed pilot-major of the Dutch fleet that sailed from Texel to explore the East Indies and South Seas. After a disastrous voyage in which they lost touch with the other four ships and over a hundred of their crew had died, Adams aboard *De Liefde* (*The Charity*) reached the coast of Japan on 19th April 1600, by which time only Adams and a few others of the crew, weakened by starvation and disease, were able to stand. They were none the less seized by the Japanese and put in confinement, though fed and cared for until they recovered.

Eventually Adams was taken to see the Shogun Iyeyasu Tokugawa and they became friends, but this meant the Shogun would not let him leave Japan. To please the Shogun Adams trained Japanese men as shipbuilders and western examples of ships were constructed for the Shogun, Adams also being employed as an instructor in gunnery, mathematics and geography. For this Adams was given a house and estate, and was even allowed to fly the Cross of St George flag from the roof. Eventually, realising he would never see Mabel, his English wife, and their two children again, to please the Shogun Adams married a Japanese woman, Magome, and they had two children who both died. One source, however, says Adams only married her because he had received a message saying Mabel was dead from a Dutch captain who had arrived off the coast of Japan. Then an English ship, the *Clove*, also arrived at Firando, Japan, in 1613 and the Shogun gave its captain John Saris a message written by Adams to James I which established trade between Japan and England.

It seems that about this time the Shogun gave Adams permission to leave Japan but Adams felt there was no point in returning now to England with his wife there dead, so he sailed in the Far East on trading voyages for the Shogun. Adams died at Yedo on 16th May 1620 and was interred on the summit of Hemmi Hill, facing east overlooking Yedo. A Dutch seaman visited Adams on his deathbed and on being told by Adams that he had left half his Japanese money to his children in England, the other half to his Japanese wife, the Dutch seaman told Adams that the earlier report had been false and his wife Mabel was still alive. Adams then had a letter drafted to give to her stating the reasons for his stay in Japan and why he could not return though he had never stopped loving her.

His Japanese wife died on 16th July, 1634, and was interred with him, there being a magnificent memorial to Adams, the 'Anjizuka' Monument in Sagiyama Park, Hemi-mura. In the meantime Adams' English wife Mabel also died, loving him till the end, and was buried in the churchyard of St Mary Magdalene church, though by some apparent mistake she is registered in the burial register as Mistress Elizabeth Adams.

Gillingham had no memorial to Adams until after an annual dinner of the Men of Kent and Kentish Men in 1926. Then the matter was raised in a speech and afterwards a committee was formed of county and local people, including the Lord Lieutenant of Kent and the Mayors of Maidstone and Gillingham and Recorder of Deal, who promoted the idea. The money was eventually raised enabling the Memorial Clock to be designed and built as a worthy monument to Adams in his birthplace. Even today visitors from Japan make a point of visiting the clock and the area where Adams was born.

Glassenbury Park

◣ In the grounds of moated Glassenbury House is a stone column. This marks the grave of Jaffa, Napoleon's favourite charger and ridden by him at the Battle of Marengo in 1800. It was named after the Battle of Jaffa Port in 1799. It is unclear how the horse came to be in this area but a General Beresford, who was in charge of the Duke of Wellington's quartermaster affairs, retired to nearby Bedgebury Park. It is possible the horse came under his control after the Battle of Waterloo and that he brought the horse to England where it ended it days in Glassenbury, dying in 1826 aged 37.

Goudhurst

There are families in Canada today who were founded by boys who had lived and been trained at Goudhurst. In the late 19th and early 20th century pioneers from Britain were emigrating to that country in search of a new life, lured by an agreement with the Canadian Government promising them enough land to be farmed or otherwise utilised to support a man and his family. In this colonization there was a shortage of skilled farm workers. One man who helped solve this problem was James Fegan, who founded Homes for Boys in several parts of London towards the end of the 19th century. At Ramsgate in 1883 he founded his first orphanage. He saw that a solution was to train suitable orphan boys in his homes and send them to Canada. He also founded Mr Fegan's Homes at Goudhurst, these being farms using imported Canadian farming equipment, with Canadian barns and other Canadian-style buildings to train these boys. When sufficiently skilled and old enough they were sent in groups of 50 to where needed in Canada. James Fegan died in 1925 and is interred in St Mary's churchyard. After his death his wife Mary became President of the Homes. In October 1943 she was killed when a German bomb hit her retirement home, and is buried with her husband.

The guide to St Mary's church is another that states its war damage (see *Farningham*). In 1940 two parachute land mines blew out most of the original glass in the church windows, except for a small panel of 15th century glass in the south aisle's west window. As in Farningham some thought at the time that this war result was beneficial, and indeed because of the loss of several undistinguished and dark Victorian stained glass windows the church is now well illuminated by natural light.

One of the terraced cottages on the slope of the village street has embedded in the brickwork of its street wall three small items of sculpture, stone mannikin figures, of a man, a woman, and an urn. The reason for the urn is a mystery; the reason for the very uncommon mannikin figures is also uncertain. Mannikin was a type of cloth produced by weavers in the Kent Weald, including those in the cottages near the church, so the figures may be a pun on the name or a form of advertisement.

In a garden in Goudhurst is an enormous tulip tree claimed to be the largest in Kent and which has a preservation order on it.

In the 1930s the road from Goudhurst to Cranbrook, via Hartley on the B2085, used to have a navigation aid for the early aircraft pilots, a lit beacon. It winked, but in foggy weather a maroon sounded, so possibly passing pilots could hear it and know approximately where they were. There was another beacon near Brenchley, probably on Castle Hill, the highest point in the area, that swept a beam around like a lighthouse.

Grain

St James' church is reputedly built on or close to the site of a pagan temple, though it is difficult to understand why there was a need at that time to erect such a building here when the Isle of Grain, jutting out into the Thames Estuary, really was an island. As a parallel to the grotesque figure in Smarden church, above the inner south doorway of St James, there is what some authorities have claimed is a pagan stone, a head with arms, that originated

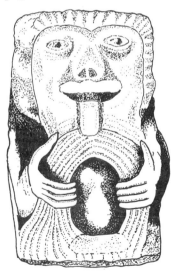

The 'Pagan' Stone, Grain church

from this temple. 'He', however, looks rather happy, not grotesque, with wide eyes, a wide smiling mouth out of which 'he' is poking his tongue. 'His' hands and well-formed fingers meanwhile appear to be pulling apart what is supposed to be his beard, a curious act, though the orifice made could be something else. The true origin is more likely that 'he' was a medieval corbel to frighten away evil spirits.

Gravesend

Gravesend's importance in the past perhaps surprisingly is that it was the first main calling place down the Thames for ships leaving London, and also the last place to unload ashore anyone who had died aboard. Gravesend's burial ground was sited between Windmill Street and Wrotham Road. Herein were interred those who had died on such ships lying off Gravesend and local, but not native-born, 'foreign' people, as it was thought unseemly to inter these two classes in the same graveyards as generations of local people. This raises a question. Pocahontas, the Red Indian 'Princess' (1595-1617) died aboard ship, either of smallpox, fever or tuberculosis, on her way back to Virginia with her husband, John Rolfe. She is, according to church records, buried 'in ye chauncell' of St George's church. But excavations in the 1920s in grave sites known to have been in the original church burnt down in 1727, and other excavations in the churchyard, discovered no remains resembling those of a young Red Indian woman, according to the famous anthropologist, Sir Arthur Keith. Could she, according to the custom, also have been interred in the parish burial ground? A letter in the *Daily Mail* in June 1923 from a reader who had been taken to Pocahontas' grave in the burial ground as a child by her grandmother, seems to confirm this possibility.

A 19th century Kent writer complained about the state of Gravesend's burial ground, '1 mile south-west of the parish church' – 'It is deeply regretted that so strong a bias persists in favour of churchyard interments and yet how often is the abode of the dead openly violated, its deposits sacrilegiously disturbed and ejected and the contents of the coffins heaped together in wild confusion. It would not be difficult to show that some of the most destructive diseases which have depopulated the human race have had their origin in the pestiferous exhalations of the overcrowded graveyard.' Graves end indeed!

One of Gravesend's former attractions that brought thousands of visitors to it by boat and railway train was Windmill Hill, off Windmill Street. The summit, about 180 ft above the level of the river at high water mark, had a windmill converted into an observatory to scan the scenery and with several houses nearby to accommodate visitors. Public houses in the vicinity had spacious pleasure grounds and tea gardens. But why did the teeming population of London descend on Windmill Hill for a day or week if it could be afforded? To breathe the pure non-smoky air of Windmill Hill.

There was a large fishing fleet at Gravesend, employed in catching herring, turbot, cod and sprats. Gravesend shrimps were also renowned. Sprat fishing commenced on Sprat Day, 9th November, the foggier the better apparently and more favourable for the fishermen to land a good haul. They *were* often landed in large quantities, and the surplus of many thousands of tons of sprats was sold as manure. In 1841 the price varied from 10d to 1/3d per bushel, but occasionally as high as 1/6d per bushel, though in 1829 the price fell to 6d a bushel. In the latter year 1,500 bushels were taken by barge up the river Medway to near Maidstone to be applied on the hop gardens at usually about 40 bushels per acre. While they were being spread around the 'hills' of hop bines probably people living in the area would have appreciated some of Gravesend's fresh air on Windmill Hill!

It is somewhat of an anti-climax that Gravesend's name has no macabre origin, despite what has been related previously. Gravesend is derived from Grove's End – 'at the grove's end', from the Old English 'graf' – grove, and Old English 'ende' – end or boundary. The park at the eastern end of Gravesend may have been the original 'graf' – grove at the 'ende' or edge of which the settlement that became Gravesend developed. It was Graveshende in 1232, before that though, in 1086, it was Gravesham, the name of the present borough.

Grove Ferry

◄|Grove Ferry, although it is closer to Upstreet, gets its name from Grove hamlet, between the Great Stour and Little Stour, and the ferry which here once plied across the Great Stour. It is unknown when the ferry was established as the principal crossing of the river below Fordwich, but certainly in the medieval period when the river was much wider and there was a need for men to cross from the

Thanet bank to the Canterbury side and vice-versa. It became a convenient crossing for smugglers running goods from the north Kent coast inland. In 1606 'undesirable elements', especially at night, were using the ferry. The Justices issued an order in July 1606 concerning 'disordered persons at times unfittinge and unlawful, who would be ferried at Grove, noe passage shall be, except in special necessity, at Grove in the sommer time after sunsett one hour, or before sun risinge one hour and so in like manner in winter tyme. If any persons were so ferried specially at night within one day after, the ferryman to give details of the persons carried, their names, where from and destination, to the local Justice of the Peace.' Failure meant a heavy fine on the ferryman.

Several are known to have been in league with smugglers in return for liquid recompense. They knew when there was a 'run' of goods and the estimated time the smugglers were to arrive at the ferry bank, so the ferry boat would be waiting to transport them rapidly across the river. If they were pursued by Revenue officers the ferryman would equally quickly return across the river, lock the chain holding the ferry boat and be in bed apparently asleep when the Revenue officers banged on his door. After being slowly aroused the ferryman would have great difficulty finding the key, in the meantime the smugglers were clear of the area.

For easier transport in the First World War the army threw a pontoon bridge across the river here but the ferry charges were still claimed by the owners of the ferry rights. At this time they were: foot passengers ½d; motorcycle, 2d; with sidecar 3d; bicycle ½d; beast ½d; sheep 6d per score; carriages, carts, wagons, motor-cars 3d per wheel. It was inevitable that increasing use of the ferry's wooden platform slowly hauled to and fro across the narrow river by a ferryman pulling on a cable would mean its replacement by a bridge, which was opened in March 1962.

About 1831 Edward W. Epps built a hotel for travellers on the south bank, calling it Ferry House. According to Bagshaw's 1847 *County Gazetteer* Epps was still landlord then, but it was known as the Rising Sun Inn and he had expanded to being also a wine, spirit and coal merchant. In 1846 the South Eastern Railway built a station opposite to the inn, on the north river bank, for the use of anglers, naturalists, wildfowlers and people with craft moored on the river. On 16th December 1945, George VI and a party of his guests arrived at Grove Ferry for duck shooting. The royal train was shunted into a siding and the king slept therein during the night guarded by a local special constable. In 1965 Southern Railway closed Grove Ferry station, everything connected with it was razed and all that can be seen today are some bricks and weed-covered rubble.

Although some of the romantic, picturesque aura of the setting near the inn was lost when the ferry was replaced it is still an attractive waterside area. The majority of people visiting it, however, are unaware of the 'hidden' story beneath their feet, that of lavender growing in Kent.

In the late 19th century a man named Bing became proprietor of the Grove Ferry Inn, as it was then called, and its ferry rights. He decided to grow lavender on the inn's land adjoining it. Seventeen acres of lavender flowers were carried into the distillery he built close to the inn. From these lavender water was distilled for sale. When he died his two daughters, Marion and Annie Bing, took over the inn and its by then 21 acres of lavender. They distilled lavender water and oil and sold it commercially in Canterbury and elsewhere. Ellen Terry, the actress living at Smallhythe, recommended it. In August when in full bloom the lavender fields must have been an aromatic, beautiful sight. Train loads of people and charabanc parties from Kent's seaside resorts came to see it, to consume lunches and teas at the inn and to walk along the river.

In 1928 disaster struck when the river overflowed its banks, flooding the lavender fields and killing the plants, which had to be replaced. Owing partly to the Depression in the 1930s the numbers of visitors fell, so did the demand for the lavender products. In July 1934 the Bing sisters were pronounced bankrupt; the inn, distillery, lavender fields being sold. Thus ended lavender growing at Grove Ferry. Successive owner-landlords have made changes to the area, but the low distillery building still survives. After the distillery equipment was removed it was used as a tea-room but is now closed. Where some of the lavender fields were is now one of the inn's car parks and the grass picnic area.

Halling

In the 19th century rectors and vicars were often in charge of only one parish. Sometimes, after caring for the needs of their church and flock, being educated men they were inclined to use their spare time to record details concerning their parish or church or both. This took various forms. Occasionally it was to record all the headstone inscriptions in the churchyard and the wall memorials and floor ledger stone inscriptions in the church. This was a valuable task as far as churchyards were concerned, recording before weather eroded the incised lettering into illegibility. Others recorded the minutiae of daily occurrences that would otherwise be forgotten in time and occasionally these collections were published to the great interest of later generations of local historians.

One such parson was Revd C.H. Fielding, compiler of *Memories of Malling and its Valley, with a Flora and Fauna of Kent,* published by Henry Oliver at West Malling in 1893.

One entry concerns the case of Henry Hawkes, a farmer at Halling. One wintry evening in 1842 he left Maidstone market to walk home. With his dog at his heels he arrived at Aylesford but there imbibed too well and was intoxicated when he set off again. However, he reached Newheed (Newhythe) and crossed Snodland Brook. The countryside was covered in deep snow and severe frost. Hawkes continued in safety reaching the Willow Walk and half a mile from Halling church. Then he staggered off the path and crossed a ditch but not realising he had gone astray he continued towards the Medway. He came to a high bank which he could not surmount, fortunately, or he would have walked into the river. With exhaustion and drink taking effect Hawkes collapsed on his back into the deep snow and fell asleep or unconscious. His dog now scratched up the snow as a sort of bank around his master, then lay on the latter's chest, the dog's body and coat providing enough warmth to keep Hawkes alive while snow continued to fall.

Next morning a wildfowler passed that way and saw the dog, who on being approached got up from his master's prone body. The wildfowler was astonished to see Hawkes who he recognised but, as he wiped away the icy snow from Hawkes' face, feared he was dead. Help was summoned and the 'body' carried to the nearest village house. Here a pulse was detected, medical assistance given and in a short time Hawkes fully recovered to tell the event. In gratitude he had a silver collar made for the dog as a commemoration of what happened. A 'gentleman', hearing of this, offered ten guineas for the dog, but Hawkes refused saying no money could buy the dog that had saved his life and he would keep it with him in luxury for the rest of its life, which he did until the dog died a natural death.

It is not a sight one expects to see in an English church but in St John the Baptist church, Halling, there is an illustration of a woman sitting up in bed. Behind this depiction, however, is a sad but true story. William Lambarde, author of the first county history, *A Perambulation of Kent,* published in 1576, lived part of his life at Halling. He married three times, two wives predeceased him. The first was 16 year old Jane Multon of Ightham, where he was living at the time, whom he married in 1570. She died in 1573 of smallpox and was interred in St Peter's church, Ightham.

The second wife was a wealthy widow, Sylvestre Dalison, née Dene, of Halling, to where he moved on marrying her in 1583. He was her second husband. They had three sons and one daughter, but she died a fortnight after the birth of twin sons in September 1587. To her memory he had what has become known as the 'Lambarde Brass' put in the church, now near the pulpit. As mentioned it depicts a woman sitting in a carved four-poster bed with her children around her, including the twins in a cradle. The inscription reads 'No lady was more full of reverence towards God than she'. In 1592 he married for the third time, another widow, Margaret Rieder, of Boughton Monchelsea, who had also been married three times. Where she is interred I know not, but she probably outlived husband William who died in 1601.

Hampton

Hampton is on the North Kent coast between Swalecliffe and Herne Bay and is now a suburb of the latter resort. Examination of an Ordnance Survey map shows a short pier there and a Pier Avenue. Formerly it also had a railway, probably the first pier railway in Britain that linked a pier with a main line railway route and perhaps the only one in the world associated with the oyster industry, but it became one of the 'lost', virtually forgotten railway routes in Kent.

A group of businessmen in 1863 purchased 30 acres of land at Hampton and founded the 'Herne Bay and Hampton Oyster Fishery Company', their area being from Swalecliffe to Reculver and three miles seaward. In the £30,000 development was included a 350 yards pier, storehouses, oyster breeding pits and a railway with goods sidings. The railway had a novel method of locomotion, sail powered with the leading wagon having a lug sail. The company's trading began on 15th September 1866, when the venture was declared open by the then Lord Mayor of London.

The 'village' of Hampton only comprised twelve cottages built by the company for its employees, and an inn. W.J. Cox in his *Guide to Whitstable and Its Surroundings,* in 1876 commented 'Hampton formerly consisted of some rude huts, the wretched habitations of a band of fishermen and smugglers, now it contains a few small houses inhabited by the employees of the Oyster Fishery Company who have built a pier at the point and laid a tramway to the railway at a cost of nearly £30,000 which has, however, proved a very profitless expenditure'.

Dredging for laid oysters was done by five oyster smacks and consignments shipped to London by the company's two yawls on Tuesdays and Fridays, when in season and weather permitting. The purpose of the railway was the simple one of being a link that allowed deliveries inland via the main Kent coast railway and also to London when required, if they could not be transported by yawl. The mainline is about three-quarters of a mile to the south of Hampton.

The coastline hereabouts, more so then than now, was subject to erosion and the aforementioned 'rude huts' and the company's twelve cottages, known as Hampton Terrace, were eventually demolished.

The pier, which was not straight but curved to westwards, was built with concrete sides infilled with the clay removed when the breeding pits were dug nearby, but after abandonment gradually the sea breached the infilling, the clay was washed away and eventually the concrete sides fell in upon themselves. Today what remains of Hampton Pier can still be viewed but should not be approached on the east side because of the depth of treacherous mud and it is wise to approach from the other side. The landward end at some time has been rebuilt by the local authority, and the clay infilling replaced with concrete. But the line of the pier is still apparent and what at first appear to be mussel-encrusted slabs and boulders are remains of the pier. Some steps on the western side lead down to a ledge that can be followed seaward to the extremity of the rebuilt pier section, then by stepping from boulder to boulder its original complete length can be followed. Surprisingly, however, among the boulders and slabs still remain lengths of the railway track where they had fallen when the pier infilling collapsed. One unfortunate effect of the pier was that of the currents causing a 'scour' of the western foreshore. To try to slow this the oyster company built defence works but eventually fresh breaches occurred. Groynes constructed also proved ineffective, so that a large area of foreshore was lost in a short time.

The Hampton Inn, formerly the Hampton Oyster Inn, still is in business on the Western Esplanade, its entrance close to the site of the railway sidings where trucks were loaded with the casks of oysters for transport to the markets. The railway track ran parallel to the small stream called the Westbrook; to the west of this were the company's five breeding pits. The pits nearest to the shore have been swallowed by the sea but the others have occasionally been used as a boating lake.

After the company's closure the rail track was lifted and removed, but was left in situ on the pier, some of the removed rails later being used in the coastal defence work hereabouts. There is no visible evidence of the track's route until the junction of the Whitstable Road opposite Westbrook Farm, now a caravan park. Here is an obvious four ft high, 14 ft wide in places railway embankment, crossing two culverts, disappearing into a ploughed field. From near this position, from a slight incline it is still possible to see the route of the line to its junction with the former London, Chatham and Dover Railway line. Near the junction there still is what appears to be the remains of a platform on which the oysters stood to be transferred to goods wagons bound for London.

Like Allhallows-on-Sea, Hampton may also be considered the intended resort that did not quite achieve this status. At the turn of the century notices on Herne Bay station stated 'Herne Bay & Hampton-on-Sea', intended to promote Hampton as a resort. Instead Herne Bay became popular and swallowed up Hampton as a suburb. But why did the oyster company fail after ten prosperous years? It appears that some of the oyster beds at least were in water too shallow and three consecutive severe winters killed a large part of the stock as it did at Whitstable. When the company failed, the railway served no useful purpose and so ended the career of the Hampton Oyster Railway.

Harbledown

➤ If you would see a depiction in glass of the original Canterbury Bells (*Campanula*) make application beforehand with the Sub-Prior of the Hospital of St Nicholas, Harbledown Hill, near Canterbury, and it is normally possible to visit St Nicholas' church, which has to be kept locked for security reasons. In a window on the north side is 14th century painted glass that has these flowers. For pilgrims who visited the shrine of St Thomas à Becket in Canterbury's cathedral, Harbledown was the last stop to see a relic of Becket, one of his shoes, before downhill into the city. Attached to the pilgrims' horses' trappings would be several small jangling bells, inscribed 'Campana Thome', as a token they were on this pilgrimage. The flowers were in fact later called by this name because they resembled the shape of the trapping bells. The window was plain glass until 1897 when a Canterbury resident, who possessed some pieces of stained glass and thought it would suit the window or part of it, contacted the Master of the Hospital. The latter agreed to see it and the fragments were found to fit the window's stone tracery, so the Master bought the glass for one pound and it was replaced into its original home in the window.

Incidentally, the term 'a canter', a small easy gallop, the gait used by horses ridden by the Canterbury pilgrims, is an abbreviation deriving from 'a Canterbury gallop'. In horsemanship, 'the hard gallop of an ambling horse; probably described from the monks and pilgrims riding to Canterbury upon ambling horses.'

The church of St Nicholas is known as 'the leper church' even now because it was founded in 1084 by Archbishop Lanfranc with a hospital for the relief of lepers' suffering, but when the need declined as leprosy disappeared in England, the hospital became the almshouses of today. Evidence of the church's early use is its floor, sloping east to west so the water ran away when the church was cleansed after a service for the lepers.

Hartlip

How pleasant to see children playing and hear them singing in the Endowed CE primary school behind the war memorial, alongside St Michael's church, for this scene is truly the heart of an English village. The school was founded by Mrs Mary Gibbon in her will of October, 1678, having given her house, garden and orchard, plus six acres of land in Hartlip to Trustees 'to put to school such poor children of the parish to be taught to read English'. Her second husband had been a vicar of Hartlip and the first school was in the vicarage garden. She also directed that 'a Bible be bought and given to each poor child when able to read any chapter in it . . . ' On this taking place the child left the school, allowing another to take their place. What is surprising is that when there were vacancies available children from as far away as Rainham, Stockbury and Newington, outside the parish, filled them.

A special school was built in 1809, then a school building was built on the present site in 1855, then rebuilt in 1906. In 1836 there were 60 children attending, all being taught to read, learn the Catechism and Collects; the girls also being taught needlework. Some children also learnt to write, if their parents were able to pay the schoolmaster for this extra instruction, which supplemented his salary from the Trustees of £36 per year. At this time Bibles were given to children during Easter, thus it appears that was when they left school, the leavers having to read aloud from the Bible in front of the vicar at a special service.

My knowledge is that this continues, and the tradition survives of the school presenting each pupil with a Bible when they leave at eleven years to progress to another school. In the Victorian period and earlier a pupil would remain at the same school for all their education until they left to start work at any age from eleven onwards. As a further encouragement but now also to keep alive the old custom the lessons are read and sidesmen's duties at the service are undertaken by the children (see *Bredhurst*).

Hawkhurst

➤Opposite All Saints church, Highgate, built 1861, is possibly one of the first shopping arcades in Kent (excepting The Pantiles precinct, Tunbridge Wells). It is an early 19th century row of properties weatherboarded above, with large shop windows under a colonnade of thin, cast-iron columns. One shop is claimed to have been 'Established 1830'.

South of St Laurence church, some parts of which are 14th century, near the large triangular green known as The Moor and close to the Sussex border, is red-brick Collingwood House. For the last 30 years of his life this was the home of Sir John Herschel, astronomer, friend of Revd Joseph Bancroft Reade (see *Bishopsbourne*). Here he died in 1871 and was interred in Westminster Abbey. A window on the south side of the church, depicting the Wise Men and the Star, is close to the pew that he used during services.

The north porch of St Laurence's church has a room over it (see *Hythe*) known in the 15th and 16th centuries as 'The Treasury', being used as a store place for valuable goods, also an office where tenants paid their rent to Battle Abbey.

Headcorn

➤The old name for this place was Hedecron. Then Queen Elizabeth visited it, was mightily pleased to see the abundant fields of corn in its boundary and said it ought to be known as Hedecorn, an anagram which stayed in use. Pronunciation, however, was Edcorn. There were other spellings, too, one in an amusing letter in the Kent County Council archives at Maidstone. It reads: 'Goodman Goomery. Whereas the parishioners of Hedcorne have had intelligence that you intend to make your habitation there, they therefore thought good to declare to you that they utterly and altogether dislike thereof and therefore desire you not to put your selfe to that trouble and charge to remove thither, for that they apprehend the lawe will not permit you to continue there without their consent, therefore would have you to prevent that trouble that will certainly ensure if you come thither. This is all from them who shall continue your friends while you remaine where you are.

Hedcorne, 30th of May, 1679

John Woollett, Avery Ramsden, churchwardens;

Matthew Porter, James Backhurst, overseers of the poor, who were backed by *nine* more signatures!

One cannot help wondering what on earth made Goodman Goomery so unwelcome. Or if he did abide by the contents of the letter. A Goodman in the Kent and Sussex speech is an old title of address to the master of the house. Goodwife applied to a man's wife, and Goody to a widow. Burial records often state, for example: 'Dec, 17. Buried old Goody Smythe'.

Herne Bay

On the seafront, sitting on a new wall facing the sea, is a larger than life fat, chubby faced, hatted stone boy, one of several sculptures commissioned by Canterbury City Council. Called 'The Boy with the Boat', and sculpted by Paula Haughney in 1993, his expression is of patient expectation as he clutches his model boat and waits for the tide to come in. This is only one feature of Herne Bay's impressive £8 million seafront scheme completed in August 1992. Almost half a mile of gardens along the new promenade are a mix of modern and old. The intention is to replicate the style of gardens that existed a century ago when Herne Bay was a popular Victorian resort visited by hundreds of holidaymaking London people. One part of the gardens is laid out in the style of a knot garden. In beds low foliage plants formulate this. There is a sculpture, a Turk's Head Knot, carved in stone by Paula Haughney and Ross Law in 1993. A modernistic metal sundial on a marble and stone column stands in Waltrop Gardens. It has the inscription 'Presented to Herne Bay by twin town Waltrop.'

Nearby is part of the old Herne Bay given a new lease of life, a weathered century-old pillar drinking fountain. A tablet one side states 'This drinking fountain which formerly stood to the east of the clock tower was re-erected on this site, March, 1993.' On the other side a tablet also there states 'Presented to the town of Herne

Bay as a Jubilee Memorial of Queen Victoria's reign by Major Horatio Davies, Sheriff of London and Middlesex 1887-8.' I wonder why many gifts to towns in the Victorian period were in the form of water use? (see *Ashford*)

The shopping streets of the resort are also well set up with sculptures. In Mortimer Street a wooden man and woman stand clutching each other while rather fearfully looking up the street. In William Street a finely detailed stone heron crouches with a fish in its beak, though it is open to doubt if a live heron could ever catch a fish in that position.

On the seafront's Central Parade is a part of Herne Bay's history before it was a holidaymaking resort, the Divers Arms. It was customary then for local fishermen to undertake other tasks to supplement fishing income, such as smuggling and securing items of salvage, not always entirely honestly. One such man was William Hooper Wood, born in Herne Bay in 1806, who first obtained a living by selling salvage. He added to his skills by becoming a 'diver' and working with others from Whitstable. In 1834 he was with them on Ireland's coast recovering goods and coins from a wreck. His share of the salvage money enabled him to buy a 'storehouse' in Herne Bay, though he continued salvaging from wrecks. In 1848, after another 'expedition' to Ireland, he was able to improve the 'storehouse' to become Wood's Beerhouse. By 1858 the name had changed to The Divers Arms with William Wood as landlord. He retired in 1861 and died in 1871, but the Divers Arms continues with an apt sign motto, for a diver, 'Where There Is Breath There Is Hope'. I wonder what Wood and his fellow wreck salvagers would think of the modern 'wreckage' – man-made sculptures of a 'Treasure Chest' by Nigel Hobbins, and the wood 'Whalebone' by Reece Ingram 1993 – deliberately cast up on the beach near the Neptune car park as part of Herne Bay's seafront revitalisation scheme?

Hinxhill

Its name is reputed to be derived from Hengist's ell, Hengist's land. This Saxon invader has been supposedly associated with nearby Kennington, 'the King's Town' and Conningbrook, 'the King's Brook', between Kennington and Hinxhill, owning land at what is now Hinxhill. Though very close to Ashford the area is still one with a low populace and scarcity of properties. This freedom of buildings and people, with winding minor roads and lanes, allows unrestricted views across countryside, and God's presence in St Mary's church can be appreciated for miles around.

North of the church is Goodcheap Farm, known originally as Godchepes, owned by a family of that surname. In 1727, over 250 years ago, instead of rural calm it was a scene of consternation that lured hundreds of people to witness in awe 'a subterraneous fire that took place in the valley near Goodcheape in this parish'. The fire started in a marshy field at the side of a little brook and continued to burn without spreading for several days. Later 'it extended itself for the space of several acres over the field, consuming all the earth where it burnt into red ashes, down to the springs, which in most places lay four feet and more deep.' It burnt for six weeks and 'consumed' about three acres of land and while doing so had 'sent forth a great smoke and a strong smell very like that of a brick kiln, but had never flamed, except when the earth was turned over and stirred up. The earth was then found to be hotter at two feet deep than at the surface. When this earth was exposed to the air, though it was very moist and not hotter than could be easily borne by the hand, the heat of it increased so fast in a few minutes it was on fire. The soil is of the same nature as that used in Holland for making turf'. In the summer of 1836, a similar fire ignited in the same place, but this time was extinguished by labourers 'throwing water thereon'.

Hollingbourne

Fortunately for Hollingbourne in the later 13th century there were no tabloid newspapers, otherwise national attention could have been focussed on the village and a scandal involving its clergy. William the chaplain in the late 1290s was accused of committing adultery with Emma Horseman. He and former chaplains were also accused of dishonesty and perjury. This probably occurred because at that time Hollingbourne's rector was John de Gaucelin, a pluralist who was also Bishop of Albano, Cardinal of SS Marcellinus and Peter, Prebendary of Driffield, rector of Hackney, Stepney, Hemingborough, Northfleet and Lyminge, so may never have visited the village. When the cat's away, etc. After a petition to him by John, Lord Cobham, about this state of affairs, a 'visitation' was held by representatives of the Archbishop, the outcome of which is unknown.

A more definite though slower outcome was that when John of

Northampton committed murder in the parish in 1304. He was charged and two years later, in 1306, was hanged on gallows that is believed to have stood on the green in front of Eyhorne Cottage.

One of the windows in All Saints church supposedly depicts the view from a bedroom window in the vicarage.

Hoo St Werburgh

Until 1968 it was known as Hoo to locals and other Kent residents alike, then it became officially Hoo St Werburgh, taken from the name of its 13th century ragstone church, which differentiates the village from St Mary's Hoo to its north-east. In Old English 'hoh' is 'a piece of land jutting out', a peninsula, ie Hoo Peninsula. In the Middle Ages it changed to Ho and eventually to Hoo and is still thus used in speech despite the addition.

It is claimed the relics of St Werburg, a Saxon princess who became a nun, were buried on the site about AD 700. Because of marauding Danes they were removed and reburied; Chester cathedral was built on the site and contained her shrine.

In 1993 a bronze plaque of St Werburg was donated by local residents, Mr and Mrs Noel O'Shea, to the Holy Family RC church, Hoo St Werburgh. It was created by Mother Concordia, a Benedictine nun at Minster-in-Thanet, whose work is in Canterbury cathedral and elsewhere worldwide. The plaque depicts the nun with a crook and Bible in one hand pointing to some geese with the other. The legend about her is that a large flock of geese were ruining crops, but no one could stop them. So the peasants appealed to St Werburg for help. She told them to 'tell the geese to come to me'. The geese were spoken to and did as they were told, leaving the crops to go to the saint who no doubt told them to improve their ways.

From 1887 to 1907 the Victorian marine artist William L. Wyllie (1851-1931) lived at the two-storey brick Victorian Hoo Lodge. It stands on one of the highest sites between Hoo St Werburgh and Lower Upnor. His studio was on the top floor, the reason being that from it he had clear views of the Medway. He spent much time on the lower Thames and Medway painting marine and coastal subjects in oil and water-colour, including harbour and dock scenes and views of the British fleet. These include *The Rochester river*, 1881; *Heave Away – barges shooting Rochester bridge*, 1884; *The Winding Medway*, 1897; *Chatham Reach*, 1904 and *A Medway Fleet*, 1906. He was also an author on painting and coastal and maritime subjects, one book being *London to the Nore*, 1905. Maidstone Museum has examples of his paintings.

Hope All Saints

On raised ground close to the B2070 Ivychurch to New Romney road, approximately half a mile from the latter place, are the fragmented walls of Hope All Saints church. It was still in use in 1541 but by 1573 was falling into disrepair and in the 18th century was a ruin, its only congregation since then being the sheep that graze in and around it. It was one of the Marsh meeting places for smugglers. In the early 19th century a Preventive Man or Riding Officer, Charles Rolfe, whose duty was supervisory in preventing smuggling, actually lay on top of one of the ruined walls listening to a smuggler gang planning a 'run' of smuggled goods from the coast and inland. Had he been caught he would have been murdered slowly, perhaps by being drowned through being held under water in a dyke, or staked out on a shore at low tide to drown as the sea came in. On this occasion the smugglers departed, Rolfe informed his superiors, and the cargo and some of the smugglers were seized.

Ruins of Hope All Saints church

Hothfield

◣ The verses on graveyard headstones can be sad, pious, prophetic, even unintentionally amusing. One of the latter is in St Mary's churchyard. Near a yew tree growing alongside a path leading to the west door of the church is the resting place of Sarah Stanford. A smallpox victim in 1790, her epitaph reads:

'Her soul without a spot is gone to Heaven;
Her spotted body to the worms is given.'

Less humorous was the fate of a Kentish landowner named Gibbes who, in the 16th century, was found guilty of an unknown crime at Hothfield. He was sentenced to be 'pressed to death'. Laid flat on his back a heavy iron weight was put on him so he was unable to move. On the first day of the sentence while still bearing the iron weight he was given three pieces of sour bread, on the second day three drinks of foul water, on the third day sour bread and so on alternately, until he died. Just one minor event in the 'good old days' (see *Fordwich*).

Hougham

◣ In 1665 the Plague occurred in Dover, large numbers of the population dying from it. As the graveyards would have been overwhelmed a piece of land was purchased in Hougham parish, on the side of a hill that fronted a pier at Lydden Spout between Abbot's Cliff, Folkestone, and Shakespeare's Cliff, Dover. Here over 900 victims were buried, the name of the land later being The Graves. Thus by such circumstances do field, wood and place names sometimes arise (see *Fordcombe*).

Hythe

◣ Writing in 1907 Walter Jerrold stated 'The neat and cheerful appearance of Hythe, which an old chronicler noted, is still remarkable. The visitor either making a stay here or passing through in leisurely fashion has several things to attract his attention. The streets run along the foot and up the slope of Quarry Hill, the connection of street with street being sometimes by long gradients and sometimes by steps . . . ' Jerrold would not find overmuch different today, apart from traffic, but it is still a well-kept town of parallel terraces and above the shop-window line is a mix of succeeding architectural periods and adaptions thereof.

The town hall in the High Street, sitting on its columns, was built in 1794. Alongside it, above head height on a narrow passage wall leading to Market Hill, is an old stone notice with the black-lettered wording 'All persons are requested to unite their Endeavours to keep this place clean and to prevent Boys or others from dirting the same'. No penalty is stated for the disregard of this by said Boys or others.

The wall of the Swan Hotel has a stone notice low down facing the pavement informing us that the distance to the hotel is 'From London Bridge 71 miles by Rochester. From Ashford 12 miles'.

Easily missed in the High Street, at head height on the left-hand side of No. 31, is a brass plate detailing the life of Sir Francis Pettit-Smith who was born there in 1808. There is also a commemorative plaque above the shop. The house was formerly called 'Propeller House' because Sir Francis invented the screw-propeller in 1836. He started as a farmer on Romney Marsh but was interested in ship propulsion, in 1835 building a model driven by a screw-propeller activated by a spring. The following year he took out a patent and built a boat which he tested at Hythe, Dover and Ramsgate. The outcome after naval tests was that the Royal Navy gave him an order for its use in HMS *Rattler*, built at Sheerness, the first screw-propelled ship in the Royal Navy. Brunel, builder of the *Great Britain*, was so impressed he changed the design of the ship from paddle to screw propulsion.

Sir Francis died in 1874 and is interred in St Leonard's church-yard several rows west of the grave of Lionel Lukin, one of the inventors of the lifeboat. There is a gravestone, but the only legible part reads 'Archimedes Pettit-Smith aged 7', this being one of his sons. *Archimedes* was the name of the first full size ship of 237 tons in which his screw-propeller was tested at Sheerness and on the Thames.

The old town hall was the parvise or apartment above the 14th century south porch of the church, being used as a council chamber in the 16th and 17th centuries until the late 18th century. It has also been used as a priest's room, school room, store room and vestry meeting place. Even today the church still rents it from the Town Council for ... 5p a year.

There are no records of Hythe ever having had an abbey, but there is a property known as The Priory opposite the south side of St Leonard's churchyard in Hillside Street off Church Hill. One of its windows is known as the 'dole window' because from it a 'dole' of bread was given out as a benefaction to the poor. Biddenden similarly also has a 'dole window', at the old workhouse, from which the Bread and Cheese Charity is handed out on Easter Monday, paid for originally by income from the local 20 acre 'Bread and Cheese Lands' (see *Westbere*).

Ickham

▬ Anyone with good eyesight or a pair of binoculars can see the unusual face of the clock which was installed on St John's church tower in 1870. Designed by Edmund Denison, who also designed Big Ben's clock, and made by Gillett & Bland, Croydon, the clock has nicks carved in the stone surround of the face instead of the conventional numbers. There is an almost identical clock at Singleton, Sussex, also made in 1870 and almost certainly made by the same firm to Denison's design specifications. So it is likely the designer approved the Ickham clock and may have inspected it after installation as he did with most church and other clocks he was involved with.

The clock face, Ickham church

Ightham

St Peter's churchyard, Ightham, pronounced 'Item', has some specimens of very early headstones, the earliest still legible being dated 1703. A clue to the age of headstones, if the inscription cannot be read, is the shorter and thicker they are the earlier they were created. These are thick and made of the hard local Kentish ragstone. In a style curious to Kent and Sussex they are shaped in outline like a human head and shoulders. The first headstones would have had a crudely incised face of the deceased, as a variation of the same custom still practised in Europe where a photograph is affixed to the headstone. What is unusual about some of the headstones is that they have profile faces, with elaborate hair styles, the same for male and female. Later the faces of the deceased were changed to a skull, even later two skulls, crossbones, scythe and spade, hourglass and other symbols of mortality, and evergreens, including laurel, cherub heads, torch, and so on as symbols of eternity.

Near the lychgate at the entrance to the churchyard is a square stone mounting block, cut with three steps. At the George & Dragon inn, Ightham Square, is another mounting block, known locally as a 'joss block' or 'jossing block', formerly used in an annual dole custom. It was called a 'joss block' because the horse was made 'to joss', Kent dialect for bringing it as close as possible to the block to enable the rider to mount (see *Crundale*).

Ivychurch

Like Brookland, St George's, Ivychurch is another Romney Marsh church that houses one of the curious sentry-box-like structures called a 'hudd', used on inclement days to protect the parson's wig and surplice from getting wet at the graveside.

The parvise or apartment above the battlemented south porch, originally the priest's room (see *Hythe*), was a secret food store in the Second World War.

For about 60 years, from 1870, the Hickman family farmed at Moat Farm, Ivychurch, and they kept pure-bred Kent Black pigs, probably one of the last instances of this breed on a Kent farm. C.F. Hickman told me that about 1918 when his father wanted to obtain a Kent Black boar for his sows he was unable to do so and was very annoyed at having to 'make do' with a Large Black boar because this meant the breed of his pigs was no longer pure. It also indicates an instance of the interbreeding that eventually meant the disappearance of the Kent Black Pig (see *Staple*).

Iwade

━━ In centuries past if they became too numerous rooks were considered to be 'vermin' (see *Eastry, Borden*), so they were culled. A rural sport was the annual rook shoot that had this alternative purpose, as well as rooks being shot for food, for they were frequently part of the rural diet. My own father ate rook pie often as a boy. One place where there was a well-known annual rook shoot was the Rookery, Iwade. In a report in the *East Kent Gazette* for May 1935, the twelve guns at the event shot 230 rooks. The reporter also added 'In view of the controversial nature of this form of sport in some quarters, it is interesting to learn from a well-informed source, that if rooks were not thinned out in some way, they would eventually cease to exist'. But not all hands were against the rook in the past. When a forebear of mine was employed as a footman for the Pomfrets of Mystole House near Chilham, Mr Pomfret refused to allow the rooks to be shot or any interference with their rookery in the elms lining the drive to the house. When he died in the 1890s and was interred in Chilham churchyard the rooks are said to have abandoned the Mystole rookery and, so my forebear claimed, nested the following year in the horse-chestnut trees around Chilham church. Perhaps they sensed the new owner of the House might not be so lenient towards rooks!

Kemsing

━━ In the early 1930s the Committee for the Preservation of Rural Kent planned to compile a Kent Domesday Book, listing every town and village, its chief or historic buildings, industries, trades, horticulture, crops, acreage, population, any known event of importance, famous persons who were born or lived there and so on. Donald Maxwell, Kent author, book illustrator, artist and ceramic tile designer, was interested in this project but also thought it should include an illustrated record of how these places looked at the time of the book's compilation. In 1933 he wrote to another organisation, the Community Council of Kent, offering to prepare a line drawing or print of each of the 350 or so villages and towns in Kent, to be kept with the book in the Council's offices or Maidstone Museum.

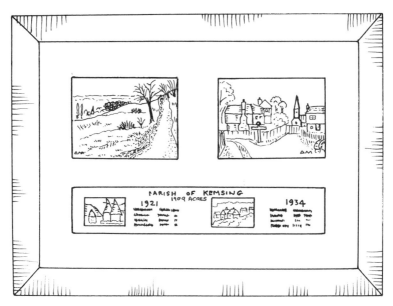

The Donald Maxwell 'Domesday' Tiles, Kemsing church

Maxwell also decided that villagers, townspeople, perhaps churches, schools, libraries and other public bodies might be interested in displaying all or some of the illustrations, perhaps of their own area, in the permanent form of ceramic tiles. Firstly he experimented with the Pembury Glazed Tile Company, then with Doulton & Co at Lambeth. Using his original coloured sketches the tiles became known as the Domesday Tiles, it being his intention to record a local scene before it changed, and as he rightly forecast, many places have. Examples of the first two, Westerham and Yalding, were given to George V, and Queen Mary was so impressed she purchased some for herself and friends. Maxwell died in 1936, but between 1933 and his death he also produced tiles for Linton, Chevening, Guston, Sheerness, Greenhithe, Kemsing, Wouldham, Halling. A clue to the identification of these tiles is his pyramidal-like initials, $\triangle$ M.

Kemsing church is fortunate that it still has its rare Maxwell Domesday Tiles, perhaps the only examples surviving in a Kent church. They are thought to have been the gift of a local benefactor, Sir Mark E. Collet. Probably made in 1935 the details are for 1921 and 1934, in the former year population was 715, in the latter 1,402; roads, houses, etc. 152 and 355 respectively, 1,909 acres in the parish, and so on. Set in a dark grey marble frame affixed to the north wall the tiles depict part of the village, Castle Bank, reputed site of Kemsing Castle (1120-1770) and St Mary the Virgin church, and the Pilgrim's Way between Kemsing and Wrotham. There are also smaller views of oasts at Heverham, a hamlet a mile east of the church and 'new houses' in Childsbridge Lane, half a mile west of the church, these being the first 'modern houses' in Kemsing.

The southern boundary of the churchyard has an uncommon 'crinkle-crankle' yellow brick wall, a continuously curving in and out or serpentine wall. They were more frequently built in the past as garden walls and provided a warm shelter for fruit trees. This Kemsing wall formerly did so for peaches and pears, now elderly residents. Built in 1922 it was also a gift of Sir Mark E. Collet, who gave land for extending the churchyard, which was bounded on the south side by this type of wall. Designed by an architect, Godfrey Pinkerton, it was constructed by a builder from Otford who enjoyed a glass of beer. So that work proceeded apace Sir Mark visited him daily to ensure the man had a plentiful supply, but this is the reason, according to local belief, that the wall is not straight.

Keston

➤ Unlike other churches Keston's small flint and stone church does not have a dedication to a saint. What it does have rather unusually, as there are few of them, is a 'weeping chancel', sited slightly to the left. The belief is that churches like this were built as an enshrinement in stone of the head of Christ as he died on the Cross falling towards the north (see *Stockbury, Cuxton, Aylesford*).

Kingsgate

➤ A property known as The Thatched House stands adjoining the North Foreland Golf Course in Elmwood Avenue. It may not be thought to have an unusual significance, but it was a pioneer in residential buildings. As an endeavour to improve the style and design of houses and cottages the *Daily Mail* sponsored the first 'Ideal Home' competition, with a £1,000 prize for what the judges decided was the best design for the 'Ideal Home'. The winning design was The Thatched House, which was built on this site as a residence for the golf club secretaries by Alfred Harmsworth, Lord Northcliffe, the millionaire newspaper proprietor and the founder of the North Foreland Golf Course in 1903. So this property at

Kingsgate can rightly be claimed to be the first 'Ideal Home' built in England, one of thousands constructed later in the 1930s and afterwards.

Kingsnorth, near Hoo St Werburgh

If William L. Wyllie (see *Hoo St Werburgh*) had been living there now almost certainly he would have painted the part of the Medway Towns' history that is berthed in Damhead Creek.

The *Medway Queen* paddle-steamer was built 70 years ago, in 1924 at the Ailsa Shipyard, Troon, for the New Medway Steam Packet Co, of Rochester. She became a familiar sight on the Medway, daily sailing from Strood Pier to Herne Bay and Southend picking up passengers at Sun Pier, Chatham, Upnor and Sheerness. She took part in the Coronation Reviews of 1937 and 1953. In 1939 she was even used to transport Medway Towns evacuees to safer areas. She was then converted into a paddle minesweeper at Deptford Creek and with a Chatham crew was part of the 10th Minesweeping Flotilla, of the Dover Patrol. Just prior to the Dunkirk evacuation, armed with a 12-pounder on the bows and machine guns on the sponsons, she was among the first ships to arrive on the French beaches and one of the last to leave. She rescued over 7,000 British and Allied servicemen. On her seventh trip she was damaged but limped back to Dover to receive the signal 'Well done, Medway Queen' from Vice-Admiral Ramsey in charge of the evacuation.

After refitting at the end of the war the *Medway Queen* returned to excursion sailings in 1947, but by 1963 cheap continental holidays caused the decline of several paddle steamers. The *Medway Queen* was laid up and offered for sale, but sadly and rather shamefully in view of her record it seemed the Medway Towns could care nothing for her fate and she was sold to a shipbreaker. However, this reached the national press and the publicity and resulting outcry caused her to be saved from this fate and she was sold for use as a marine clubhouse on the river Medina, Isle of Wight. This was not to be a happy ending for her there. After several years she was replaced by a larger ship and while being moved the *Medway Queen* was accidentally sunk and was allowed to become an abandoned hulk for some ten years.

In 1984 some ship enthusiasts brought her back to the Medway on a pontoon but attempts by her new owners to preserve her were unsuccessful. Moored to the wall of St Mary's Wharf, Chatham Dockyard, for the second time she sank and was abandoned. But in 1985 a Medway Queen Preservation Society was formed by other enthusiasts who could not bear to see her rot away. After removing tons of mud from her by hand buckets and making her watertight enough to float over two tides as required by the authorities before they would allow her to be towed down-river, the *Medway Queen* was moved to a berth that had been generously offered at Damhead Creek, Hoo Peninsula; ironically on the site that originally had been used by a shipbreaking company. The Society, a registered charity, now owns the ship and all the signs for her are now good. This happy outcome warms the heart of the author, who as a Medway Towns boy often saw her sailing down the Medway, including the very last day she carried passengers.

A marine survey has been encouraging, a business and fund-raising plan established with the intention to restore the *Medway Queen* to a revenue-earning condition again. A generous grant from Rochester-upon-Medway Council had enabled plans to be made for this to become reality, though in the future rather than immediately. Then she will no longer be 'hidden' as it were in Damhead Creek but again a familiar sight on the Medway.

Visitors are welcome on Thursdays and Saturdays, 10 am to 4 pm, the ship's berth in Damhead Creek is reached via the main gate to the Kingsnorth Industrial Estate, Stoke Road, Kingsnorth, near Hoo St Werburgh and the power station. From the A2 follow the A228 towards Grain and turn off at Kingsnorth Power Station. If coming from afar it is advisable first to contact the Society on 01634 252848 to ensure members are there to receive visitors.

The industrial estate was formerly the site of airship development in Kent. Some of the original buildings are still standing but are rapidly being replaced during development of the area. Faced with war and a threat from German airships, in 1913 work started constructing an airship shed, and was completed in June 1914. In 1915 the Admiralty ordered that the Kingsnorth station should design and build a special airship, the Submarine Scout, as its name indicates for use in patrolling on the lookout for German submarines. After the first airship, SS1, successfully flew on its maiden flight in March 1915 it was used by the Royal Naval Air Service. Kingsnorth was expanded as its development of airships proceeded, with more airship sheds, fabric workshops, power house and experimental laboratories, also attached being a special railway line and riverside pier. Over 150 airships of several types had been built by the end of the First World War.

In 1920, with postwar economies, Kingsnorth's facilities were transferred to Cardington, Bedfordshire, and Kingsnorth closed. The

323 acre site was abandoned until in 1930 it was bought by Berry Wiggins, an oil refining company. Now the site is dominated by Powergen's giant electric power station. Even so, in the vicinity there are still World War One pillboxes and remains of the Hundred of Hoo railway line to be discovered.

Lamberhurst

◤ Formerly Lamberhurst was the centre of the Wealden iron-smelting industry. It was here, about a mile west of the village, at Gloucester Furnace, now called Furnace Mill, that the iron railings of St Paul's, London, were cast. Between 1710 and 1714 they were transported by river on the Medway and up the Thames to their destination. In 1976 some came back to their place of origin to be placed beside the village hall. There is a small plaque on a wall stating 'These railings were cast at Lamberhurst for St Paul's in 1710 and stood there for over 200 years. They were returned to Lamberhurst in 1976 by Dean and Chapter of St Paul's and erected by the parish council in 1979'. The water to operate the hammers, etc at the foundry was brought from the river Teise by a feat of 16th century water engineering, a form of canal or cut. There was a straight length for about 1,300 yards to avoid a bend in the Teise, and a specially built levee. The stonework in the bank and bottom of the river is still there. The adjoining Pond Field was formerly a man-made three acre pond to hold extra water. The site of hammer ponds at the mill can still be found there and iron lumps in the woodland.

Another craft in Lamberhurst was cloth weaving and a line of timbered houses up the hill of the village street was called The Weavers Stair, demolished since the Second World War for council houses. The village also had Smith's Brewery with a watermill that drove a generator, the surplus electricity being sold to Seeboard for use in the village. On the opposite side of the river to the iron foundry is a steep bank and local tradition states it was specially built up for the testing of the Gloucester Furnace-made cannons, which were fired at it. The output of the furnace at its peak were cannons for the navy under government contract.

Unwisely the owners also illicitly cast cannons for French privateers, these being smuggled to France; smuggling in reverse. This 'trade' was discovered, the owners heavily fined and they lost the government contracts, a circumstance that helped hasten the end of this furnace.

At the entrance to Furnace Mill Farm is a property with a large pond, called Mill Place or the Pepper Mill, but it is unknown if peppercorns were ever milled there and where they could come from to be so used. Possibly an owner long ago was surnamed Pepper.

Lenham

➤ In centuries past when a misdemeanour required punishment more severe than a period in the stocks the culprit, sometimes a runaway 'inservice' labourer, was 'housed' in the local lock-up to await judgement of magistrate or judiciary. Most large communities had such a property and Lenham still has its lock-up in the Faversham Road. It is rather attractive now, though perhaps not to past inmates, with its ashlar front and rusticated arch, at the end of the short cobbled and grassed street of 18th century red-brick cottages. According to Sir Charles Igglesden's *Saunter Through Kent*, Vol I, it is not as old as it appears: 'Opposite [the Douglas Almshouses] is a solid stone construction, apparently of great age, but as a matter of fact it was built at the beginning of the present [19th] century for the purposes of a lock-up. At the present time [1900] it is used as a mortuary.' Not now.

Littlebourne

➤ On the Littlebourne to Fordwich road, just over a mile north-eastwards from Littlebourne's large Green, is Elbridge House lying in a rural hollow. For several generations it was the residence of the Denne family, landowning lords of the manor of Littlebourne. One member was Major Henry William Denne of the Gordon Highlanders, who died in 1900 in the Boer War. At the battle of Elandslaagte a bullet first passed through a corporal's helmet and then hit Major Denne in the head, fatally injuring him. Queen Victoria learned of the tragedy and offered his pregnant wife and her two young children apartments in Hampton Court and when the baby was born two months after its father's death Queen Victoria was godmother.

In our conservation-minded days an earlier member of the Denne family who owned Elbridge, Henry Denne (1755-1822), would not be kindly thought of. Among his interests was shooting game and other wildlife. He kept a record and between 1770 and 1809 shot 753 pheasants, 2,322 partridges, 2,079 hares, 3,764 rabbits, 1,682 woodcock, 2,552 snipe, 600 'wildfowl', 700 landrail and two eagles.

In his will he requested to be carved on his table tomb 'The game I killed in my sporting days from the first day I carried a gun till the last. On the head the first eagle I shot in 1770 and on the foot the second eagle shot in 1797. On the side all the feathered tribe in detail each sort and on the other side the fur and flesh animals.'

Although he had been a churchwarden and lord of the manor this request was not granted. He was only allowed to have the two perched black eagles carved, each in a cartouche, one each end of his table tomb. He was interred on the north side of St Vincent's churchyard, with his two wives – first, Sarah Hollingbury aged 17, who died in 1809; second, Elizabeth Whittle, aged 79, who died in 1836. He had also requested in his will that on her death his second wife was to be interred with him and his first wife in the same table tomb which was to be enlarged to hold all three of them if necessary, and therein they are together today.

Alongside is the tall memorial stone on the grave of Adela Wyman, daughter of an Inca princess (see *Gravesend*). A local man named Wyman travelled to Peru in the 19th century, married an Inca princess who gave birth to a daughter. The daughter visited her father's home in 1862, was taken ill, probably with tuberculosis, and died in 1864 aged 16.

Lower Halstow

➤ As you leave the village and travel towards Funton and Isle of Sheppey, St Margaret's church is on the left. Behind a brick wall on the right is an old property, Stray House, with the equally old Stray Cottages near Stray Orchard a short distance further on. A small stream that passes under, formerly over, the road to empty into Halstow Creek is called the Stray. Originating as a ditch draining the nearby Callum Hill, now it is often dry in summer. It is also not to be confused with the other stream passing through the village, known in the 19th century as the Libbett. That originates from springs at Newington to the south which have also been drying up in summer for several years.

The name 'stray' is very old in this context. The OED defines 'stray: of a stream to meander; the stream that meanders'. In 1591 Shakespeare in *Two Gentlemen of Verona*, Act II, Sc vii, 31 wrote: 'And so by many winding nookes he [the current] straies to the wilde ocean'. In 1700 Dryden, in his *Acis & Galatea*, line 78, wrote: 'More clear than ice or running streams that stray through garden plots'.

The Isle of Grain and Hoo Peninsula are separated by a stream called the Stray, the northern end having North Yantlet Creek, the southern end Colemouth Creek. Wider and deeper small vessels used the Stray to avoid going around the outer seaward side of the island.

Lower Halstow and local barges have several times been used for cinema films. Before postwar development overtook the idyllic creekside setting, sailing barges docked in Halstow Dock close by the church. The *Wiltshire*, one of the barges of Eastwoods the brickmakers, was used in 1938 in *Sailing Along* starring Jessie Matthews and Sonny Hale. In 1937 Eastwoods' *Surrey* was renamed *Heart in Hand* for a film *Beauty and the Barge*, starring Gordon Harker and a very young Ronald Shiner. *Surrey* was also used in *Red Sails in the Sunset* again starring Jessie Matthews. Many of the location scenes were shot at Otterham Quay and Lower Halstow. There was also a John Mills' film shot on wrecked concrete barges at Funton Creek in the 1950s.

Lower Hardres

◄ Wall memorials in churches tend to have glowing sentiments paying honour to the deceased, which is understandable, though the reader cannot help sometimes wondering if in life the person so described could possibly have been so saintly and benevolent. James Tillard, of Street End House, Lower Hardres, was. The terms of his £3,000 Benefaction in his 1827 will displayed in the church's south porch confirm this, but it was also he who paid for the church to be rebuilt. The original 13th century church was a small structure, with two side aisles and a low pointed steeple. It is uncertain why the church was replaced. It may have been damaged by fire or was in such disrepair it would cost too much to restore. Alternatively was it too small and an increasing population meant a larger building was needed? Perhaps James Tillard just wanted a 'modern' church and had the money to pay for it. Whatever the circumstances he expended £2,000 for the erection of this church in Early English style with its lofty octagonal steeple and spire. A notice in the church states it was built 'about 1820' and generous Mr Tillard gave a set of communion plate dated 1824, though authorities on churches persist in stating it was erected 1831-1832.

Tillard died in 1828 and was buried in his own church according to his wall memorial tablet near the wide chancel. Bagshaw's *Gazetteer*, 1847, commented 'The whole fabric has a neat and pleasing appearance'. A 20th century writer, however, has described it as 'ugly'. He cannot have seen it in its setting when the east and south sides of the churchyard are white with flowers so that it rivals Hinxhill for the title of 'the church of the snowdrops'.

Lydd

➤ In All Saints churchyard there is a 'grave' without a body. Edward Greenland was born in Lydd and baptised on 9th January 1853, the son of Edward and Henrietta Greenland, who altogether had eight children. The Greenlands were an old established Lydd family, parish records for them dating back to 1686. The memorial cross and tombstone on the 'grave' has the inscription 'Sacred In Memory of Edward Greenland who fell from the rigging of HMS *Barosa* off Yokohama and was drowned on the 28th February 1870, aged 17 years. This stone is erected by Lieut. C.E. Drake of HMS *Barosa* as a mark of esteem and regret felt by himself and the crew'. But the Lydd burials register does not include entry details of the interment of Edward Greenland, so it has to be assumed the grave is empty. Yet it was obviously locally thought pertinent in the light of the Greenland family's old establishment in Lydd, to allow this form of memorial cross and tombstone to be thus placed in the churchyard (see *Whitstable*).

In 1940 the huge church, known as 'the cathedral of Romney Marsh', was hit by a bomb which destroyed the chancel and damaged the chapels and roofs. The damage is shown in a painting under the tower inside the west doorway. Some of the church's original Caen stone was saved for reuse, but recovered stone from the bombed precincts, with that from several churches and other bomb damaged buildings of Canterbury, was used to totally rebuild the chancel of Lydd church in 1958, so that out of destruction came forth a continuing usefulness.

Lympne

➤ The numerous boots and shoes of Lympne children walking on Isaac Bachelour's marble floor slab on their way to school in the north aisle of St Stephen's church have worn away the lettering. Kent guide books often state it was an 'interesting epitaph and verse but too long to give here'. So I will do so. It read 'Here lieth interred the body of Captain Isaac Bachelour who being commissioned to serve His Majesty under the honourable title in the Militia for the

County was discharged to death the 26th May, 1684 (1?) aged 40; whose sorrowful widow, Mrs Mary Bachelour, as a pledge of respect to his surviving memory, placed this stone for an imperfect monument of his desert and her affection:

> Since a life-vanquished Captain here doth lie
> Death hath a sting and grave a victory,
> But hold! Can he be vanquished whose last breath
> Challenged the grave and triumphed over death?
> No, but he changed his quarters and marched on
> To meet the Captain of his salvation
> Under whose more auspicious command
> He is now commissioned in a better land,
> Where soldiers are all Saints – Heaven is the prize
> And prayers and praises the sole exercise.
> Thus fights our Captain and proclaims his cause
> In thundering peals of Halleluias.'

Near the church's lychgate, at the end of the churchyard wall, there are some mounting steps (see *Crundale*), but it is not likely Captain Bachelour made use of them.

Maidstone

➤ It is a surprise to find a part of the old House of Commons preserved in Maidstone's Brenchley Gardens at the north end of the town near Week Street. On 10th May 1941 during the German bombing of London, the Debating Chamber of the House of Commons was destroyed. One of the tall finials (the tops of pinnacles) that had crowned the main wall was donated to Maidstone in 1948 by Alfred C. Bossom, MP, who on the 18th June that year had represented the borough in Parliament for a longer period than any previous MP. Brenchley Gardens themselves were donated to the town by Julius Brenchley in 1873. The same benefactor also gave valuable objects concerning the ethnography of the South Sea Islands and arts of China and Japan now to be seen in Maidstone Museum.

In the same gardens stands another reminder of London. Near the finial is a cenotaph to the dead of the Queen's Own Royal West Kent Regiment. Sir Edwin Lutyens, architect of the famous cenotaph in Whitehall, also designed this smaller size replica, about two-thirds the London monument. On two sides is the inscription: 'The Glorious Dead of the Queen's Own Royal West Kent Regiment' and on the other two the dates MCMXIV and MCMXIX. In spring

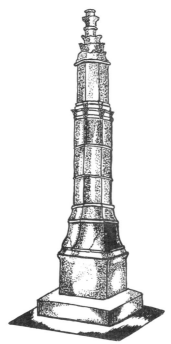

Eroded finial from Houses of Parliament
now in Brenchley Gardens, Maidstone

1921 it was ready to be unveiled but owing to a coal strike, mobilisation of the Defence Force and other circumstances, the ceremony was not held until 30th August 1921.

If visitors to Maidstone look above shop front level they will note some of the town's examples of pargeting. This is a form of plasterwork with patterns, ornament, figures, etc, either in relief or engraved in it. On 78 Bank Street is a fine example dated 1611. On the left side are the Arms of Henry, Prince of Wales, feathers, etc, on the right the Arms of England, while centrally under a window is much florid foliate work. Nos. 55-57 Week Street on two upper storeys have pargeting dated 1680 with the letters SP. Though less majestic than the Bank Street example this one has swags − hanging foliage wreaths or festoons − between pilasters or columns, with other ornamentation.

On Rocky Hill, London Road, adjacent to the Employment Service offices, stands a large spreading cedar tree. Maidstone Museum possesses a lead plaque that was attached to it, reading 'This cedar was planted by the founder of the firm 1796'. The man referred to was James Bunyard, founder of Bunyard and Company, formerly renowned as seedsmen and nurserymen in the horticultural world. Even today there are varieties in cultivation that were bred by this family, who had nurseries in Maidstone, Allington and Ashford. One example is the cooking apple, Grenadier, corrupted in lazy Kent speech to Granada, introduced by James' grandson George about 1860. Another is Bunyard's Exhibition broad bean, still grown and recommended.

James Bunyard, almost certainly born in the town, trained and worked as a gardener at Hampton Court for George III and George IV. Then he became head gardener for the Earl of Romney at Mote Park, Maidstone. In 1796 he bought some land in West Borough, Maidstone, and started as a florist and nurseryman. He propered and rented more land. One of his customers was Lady Hester Stanhope, the traveller who for a time kept house for her uncle William Pitt and bought trees to grow on the bare slopes surrounding Walmer Castle. James died in 1844 and is interred near the vestry entrance in All Saints churchyard, Maidstone.

James' second son Thomas (1804-1880), took over the still expanding business with more land and greenhouses in the area, and bought a nursery at Ashford. He introduced a new fuchsia, then a novelty plant, called Duchess of Kent, popular for being one of the first large, white-sepalled varieties. In 1855 his second son, George, joined the business which by now was nationally famous. In 1881 they had over 500 varieties of fruit trees in their catalogue, also selling evergreens, bush fruits, herbaceous plants, native tree saplings, ferns, vines and roses. An odd diversion was having six acres of land at the Chiltern Hundreds, Penenden Heath, to grow wood for walking sticks. To compete with other firms, such as Laxton and Rivers, Bunyard introduced many new varieties. Not only was he expert on apples and pears but also figs. It was his opinion that the old variety Reculver growing in Kent, called later Black Provence, was named after the town Reculver and introduced through the port, probably as dried fruit containing seeds, which the Romans planted around their Kentish villas.

In 1912 he listed his own bred dessert apple, Maidstone Favourite, like a Beauty of Bath but firmer textured. The principal apple he bred, however, is the Allington Pippin, a late autumn dessert apple, still available from specialist fruit tree nurseries. George died in 1919 and is interred in St Laurence's churchyard, Mereworth. The business continued in the family, who exhibited 60 apple varieties at the 1932 Chelsea Flower Show. In 1939 the Allington nursery and fruit ground was sold to a farmer to produce war effort food. Bunyard's other nurseries went over to growing lettuce and other food plants, though the seed and apple tree trade continued.

In the late 1950s the land on Rocky Hill was sold. A catalogue was issued in 1963 and offered new flower varieties including a new zinnia. By the end of the 1960s it was obvious the former style of business could not continue viably and George Bunyard and Co was sold. Laxton bought all the fruit stock, Cuthberts the seed section. The Bower Mount Road nursery site is now covered by executive-type houses. Their former garden shop and head office at the junction of London Road and Tonbridge Road, Maidstone, became a tool hire firm's premises. The cedar tree, however, remains as a living memorial to this Maidstone family's involvement in horticultural history.

Marden

Near the two-storeyed south porch of St Michaels and All Angels church are some old parish stocks (see *Fordwich*), originally sited outside the wooden lock-up (small gaol) in the village square, but moved here for safety. They were presented by 'E. Hussey, Lord of the Manor 1882'. It seems likely these are therefore replicas as it is doubtful if malingerers and other petty criminals were being thus punished in the stocks in the late 19th century. Some would say, however, they ought to be reintroduced and used everywhere as there is no greater deterrent than ridicule from one's fellow men and women!

Margate

One of the world's smallest theatres can be seen and visited at 2a Eastern Esplanade in Cliftonville, Margate. How it came into being is a true story, the stuff of theatrical aspirations. The building was built as a coach house in 1896. Eventually, as cars became more numerous, it was converted into a double garage. By 1984, however, the building had fallen on hard times and was rapidly becoming derelict. It was then Lesley Parr-Byrne, a former theatrical agent, and her TV and film actress daughter Sarah, came on a shopping excursion to Margate. They saw the 'For Sale, Freehold, Garage, Flat and Forecourt' and stopped. Lesley had nurtured a dream of one day owning her own theatre, but the large sum that would be required seemed to put it beyond achievement. However, they decided just to look inside, no harm in that. They viewed everything and strangely did not see a dark, decrepit, typical car-smelly garage, but a tiny Victorian theatre, red and gold, conveying the atmosphere of music hall variety and drama of those far-off days. They went home, sold their house and bought the Esplanade property. One of them said 'Why, it's no bigger than your thumb!', so they called it The Tom Thumb Theatre.

Skilful conversion turned it into a licensed public theatre seating 60 people with the smallest stage of any public theatre in the world, measuring seven ft by ten ft. Without stairs, it is popular with senior citizens who enjoy its shows. The exterior has a charming wood upper storey with a balustrade, and the dressing room is in a wooden chalet built on the back! The Tom Thumb won a civic award in 1985.

There is a summer season and a pantomime, the summer shows linked with history and nostalgia, from the life of Tutankhamun, the story of the six wives of Henry VIII, to a tribute to the musicals of the 1930s, 40s, and 50s. The history is painlessly related with much jollity to musical accompaniment. The cast are all professional actors and actresses who appear only for petrol expenses, the theatre being run through donations or by patrons becoming 'Friends of the Tom Thumb'. The delight in this lush and fascinating Victorian theatre atmosphere is completed by each member of the audience receiving an interval glass of sherry and a chocolate and leaving for home with a souvenir.

Less fortunate is the pre-war and post-war summer season, sea front venue, nearby Cliftonville Lido, where performances are no longer held. One of the stars there in the 1920s and 30s was Albert Fuller, who as 'Leslie Fuller', was actor, entertainer and concert party comedian. Regularly he appeared in a show *The Peddlers* at The Lido. He also acted in cheap British film comedies, making 26. Probably the best known is *Not So Quiet On The Western Front* in 1930. He died in 1948 and is interred in Margate's St John's cemetery, Manston Road.

Another 'show business' personality associated with Margate is 'Lord' John Sanger, circus proprietor and showman. He died in 1889. As befits a 'showman', Lord John Sanger's grave is marked by a marble plinth on which stands an almost full-size white circus horse in mourning, easily seen from a considerable distance across the cemetery. In the same cemetery he is surrounded by other members of the Sanger circus family, including 'Lord' George Sanger, who died in 1911. Lord George's winter circus headquarters was the Hall-By-The-Sea, Margate, later part of the grounds of what is now 'Dreamland'.

Meopham

Shortly after the Second World War ended Meopham, pronounced Meppum, was scheduled to become a new satellite town of London, but the scheme was abandoned and the planners chose elsewhere (see *Cliffe, Eynsford*).

Writing in 1907 Walter Jerrold in *Highways & Byways in Kent,* said of Meopham 'Here we should pause to remember that in this village was born in 1608 John Tradescant the Younger, the famous botanist and traveller whose *Closet of Rarities* forms part of the Ashmolean Museum at Oxford. Tradescant and his father deserve our grateful remembrances for the many trees and plants they introduced into this country, trees and plants so familiar now that it is difficult to realise what our gardens (and especially our suburban gardens) would be without them, for among the trees which we owe to them are the acacia, the plane and the lilac.'

John's birth occurred here because in 1607 John Tradescant the Elder was appointed gardener to the Earl of Salisbury, who held the nearby manor of Shorne. John came over on a visit, liked the look of a Meopham girl, married her and settled down, later to become gardener to Henrietta Maria, Charles I's queen, a job in which his son was later to succeed him. Probably the best known of their plant introductions to be seen as standby greenery on many a Kent windowsill is the trailing *Tradescantia virginia.*

In numerous churches memorial brasses are missing from their matrix in the floor ledger stones on grave sites. It is assumed this is because metal thieves steal them. This might not, however, be true of all the missing brasses. In 1797 Hasted recorded the case at Meopham within the memory of several elderly people in the parish that when some of the bells were being recast it was found there was insufficient metal for the purpose. So 'some persons tore off the brass inscriptions from the stones in this church, except that of Follham and threw them into the heating metal to add to its quantity'. Probably the reason why the bell-founders ignored the brass plate for John Follham, who died in June 1455 is he was a vicar and they could hardly use the metal from the grave of a man of the cloth even if it was for bells for his church.

Mereworth

➤ In one part of Kent and possibly elsewhere a group of wild boar have recently re-established themselves, most likely after several escaped from captivity in a wildlife park or a farm where they were being bred for their meat. Formerly the boar was a natural inhabitant of wooded areas in Kent. According to the Twysden MSS Mereworth was possibly the habitat of the last survivors: 'Towards the north this parish rises up to the ridge of hills, called the Quarry Hills (and there are now in them, though few in number several of the Martin Cats) over which is the extensive tract of woodland called the Herst Wood (Hurst Wood) in which so late as Queen Elizabeth there were many wild swine, with which the whole Weald formerly abounded, by reason of the plenty of pannage from the acorns throughout it.' 'Martin cat' or 'marten cat' was the original name for the pine marten, now restricted to Wales, the Lake District and Scotland. The boar became extinct in Kent, hunted for its flesh and because of the damage it caused uprooting woodland floors. The pine marten, being carnivorous, was killed by gamekeepers and also by hunters for its fur.

Milton Regis

➤ Every boy and girl, past and present, who has had bonfires and fireworks knows who Guy Fawkes was – one of the Gunpowder, Treason and Plot conspirators. But who was Simon Gilker? Few now remember him, but in an indirect way he was involved as a result of the outcome of this villainy. Fortunately, too, someone in the past did want him to be remembered. They erected a headstone on his grave across the path from the porch of Holy Trinity with St Paul church. So we thus know that according to it he 'was killed by means of a rockett November 5th, 1696, aged 48'. Gilker was the local Administrator of the Poor Law among other duties. Not a job likely to bring you many friends in the community in those days. The event that caused his death is unknown but the 'rockett' was probably a ship's signal rocket set off from a navy ship at Sheerness or nearer in the Swale or perhaps even at Milton Regis, a royalist port. Because of the significance of the date of death he may have been witnessing some form of shipboard commemoration from the shore, or attending a local celebration, when the 'rockett' went off course. It is improbable, even in his official capacity, he would have been 'liberating rocketts' for the occasion. Maybe he was just the unlucky bystander. Whatever the circumstances it seems that in 1696 Simon Gilker became the first firework casualty in England.

Mottingham

Near Mottingham railway station is the Tarn. Today it is classed as a small natural lake surrounded by woodland and gardens, purchased by Woolwich Borough Council in 1935, who carried out major improvement work to it. The name, the Tarn, was being used by 1903, but before that it was known as 'Starbucks Pond'. There has been speculation that the Tarn was originally stocked with fish to supply banquets at nearby Eltham Palace, as this would have been the nearest area of water for this purpose, apart from the palace moat. That may have been a use to which it was put, but what was the origin of this stretch of water? A natural lake may have formed in a suitable area of land over a period of time. Or was it created all in one day?

Before the Westerham 'astonishing scene' of 1596 (which see) another similar event took place here. 'A marvellous accident happened on August 4th 1585 in the Hamlet of Mottingham (pertaining to Eltham in this county) in a Field which belongeth to Sir Percyval Hart [of Lullingstone Manor, who survived serving Henry VIII, Edward VI, Mary I, Elizabeth I, to die in his bed there aged 84]. Betimes in the morning the ground began to sink, so much that three great Elm trees were suddenly swallowed into the Pit, the tops falling downward into the hole and before ten o'clock they were so overwhelmed that no part of them might be discerned, the Concave being suddenly filled with Water. The compasse of the hole was about 80 yards and so profound that a sounding line of fifty fathoms could hardly find or feel any bottom. At about 10 yards distant from the above there was another piece of ground which sunk in like manner near the highway and so near a dwelling house as to terrify the inhabitants of it.' Thus wrote Thomas Fuller (1608-1661), who may possibly have based his account on the memories of elderly eye witnesses. Incidentally, Hasted in his Vol I, 1797, uses Fuller's account verbatim. After such a length of time the Tarn/Starbucks Pond would have silted in, but I wonder if during its history anyone has ever plumbed its depth? Could the Tarn and the 1585 event be connected and one and the same?

Murston

➤ Now a suburb of Sittingbourne, Murston is unusual in that its church is in two parts. The 'new' church, built in 1873, but incorporating some of the original windows, columns and screen, can be seen at one end of the street as the visitor enters Murston, while the chancel of the old church is on an open green, three-quarters of a mile further north.

The original Murston church had as one of its rectors Revd Gawin Hyereck from 1583 to 1614. In the days of walking or using horse transport it was customary to ride a horse to church to attend services and leave the horse outside (see *Crundale*). Hyereck was summoned to appear before the Canterbury Consistory Court on 24 charges, the 18th charge being that he took his horse into church during services, not only on 'week daies' but also on 'Sundaies' and 'holidaies'. When the horse whinnied as the rector preached he told the congregation that 'the horse did laugh at the Word of God to the imminent and apparent danger of his own soul'. It is not recorded what happened to the eccentric Revd Hyereck, perhaps admonishment and removal elsewhere. He was not unfrocked as he was afterwards rector of St Mary's church, Hoo and vicar of St Peter's church, Bredhurst, where he died in 1657 and is interred in the church.

Newchurch

➤ What's in a surname? Matthew Tumble was repairing the tower of St Peter and St Paul church in 1850 when he fell from it and was killed. Out of respect for his memory the local school was closed for the day and the children attended his funeral service. At the base of the south side of the tower, about centre and looking over the dyke and playing field, there is a stone marking the spot where it happened, the stone now level with the earth bearing the year '1850' but no name.

Newington-by-Folkestone

➤ On the B2065 between Etchinghill and Newington, on the left-hand side and before approaching the awe-inspiring or awful (whichever your point of view) Channel Tunnel conurbation, stands

'Eyecatcher' – Temple Cottage, Newington-by-Folkestone

an 'eyecatcher'. It is known as Temple Cottage, but it is more imposing and larger than a cottage. It is an 18th century folly (see *Sevenoaks*) but in the form of and used as a dwelling. In two storeys, it has a Gothic façade with eleven Gothic windows and a door; on the roof there is a central octagonal lantern. The stone to build it came from a medieval house demolished at Brockhill, a reuse of materials. This type of building was built in the landscape as an 'eyecatcher' and this one can be closely seen from the road.

Northbourne

Northbourne Court, west of Deal, has three tiers of brick terraces flanked by massive high walls built with ten-inch bricks. These terraces and walls are an unusual architectural feature of Northbourne Court, a rarely surviving characteristic of Tudor gardens. The terraces are a form of mount up which people could ascend to view the countryside beyond the walls, a simple version of the gazebo (see *Faversham*). Only a few of this type of mount survive in England. The gardens are open fortnightly on Sundays in summer and autumn so visitors can also view inside the gardens, their speciality being old-fashioned flowers and grey foliage plants that thrive on chalk soil.

Within Northbourne parish is the hamlet of Finglesham. According to a Kentish saying couples living together as man and wife but not officially wed were 'married in Finglesham church', there being no church at Finglesham.

Northfleet

Now included in the Borough of Gravesham Northfleet has an industrial history, papermaking, chalk extraction, lime burning, etc, so the area would seem an unlikely one to choose as a site for a pleasure resort. However, when industry was a lesser feature of Northfleet one Jeremiah Rosher in 1835 planned a riverside estate called Rosherville. Rosher was a director of the Rosherville Pier Company founded to build a pier on the Thames at Northfleet. The company bought 20 acres of land that formerly had been a chalk pit, and at a cost of over £25,000 converted it into a site the *London Journal* called 'The *beau-ideal* of all the ruraliser can desire'. According to one report 'many thousands of choice trees and shrubs, including a fine collection of American plants and exotics, have been planted. On entering Rosherville's Botanic Gardens, the visitor walks along a winding path and arrives at the Italian Garden, a large tract of land laid out in classical fashion, having an ornamental fountain with a vase and Triton supported by dolphins. A Pleasure Lawn is surrounded by luxuriant foliage and bold cliffs, the striking effect of the Embattled Tower making this part of the Gardens particularly interesting. At the base of the Tower is the Banqueting Hall holding six hundred people. To the left there is a Bear Pit, a broad gravel walk, passing the Monkey House and the Aviary, that leads to the Archery Ground. The Ponds form a picturesque feature with many rare species of aquatic birds. The Mount [see *Northbourne*] on the right of the Bear Pit rises among the shrubs and plants and from it the Italian Garden can be seen to advantage. The Maze is a source of excitement to young visitors. On Gala Days the Gardens are illuminated and there is music and dancing until 10 at night, which is concluded by a firework display.' Admission, however, had to be paid for – 6d (2½p) per adult, annual season tickets available at 10 shillings (50p). This did not deter the London population coming by paddle steamer to Rosher's pier or by railway train to Northfleet's new station. With modifications what a tourist attraction the gardens would be today, but all is gone except the name, and Jeremiah Rosher, lying in St Botolph's churchyard, is himself forgotten like his once fashionable resort gardens.

Old Romney

It comes as a surprise but not unpleasing to the eye of the visitor to Old Romney's church to see the Georgian horse box pews and the pillared 18th century minstrels' gallery painted pink. Originally they were grey, but in the 1960s the Rank film company used the interior during the making of the film *Dr Syn* on Romney Marsh. They also replaced the worn unsteady stairs to the gallery. At the end of filming the cheque for the use of the church paid for vital repairs to make watertight the roof, and it was decided to leave the pews as they are today.

Following a practice in other Romney Marsh villages formerly, some of the graves in the grassed churchyard had curved, grave-length, metal frameworks over them, resembling wire cloches, with a central part where the grave tender could get access to weed the grave and place flowers, then close it again. The intention was that when sheep were put in the churchyard to graze, they were prevented from browsing on the grave flowers and plants. These metal protectors have all gone but several graves have railings, possibly to serve the same purpose as well as outline the grave, though a determined sheep might thus feed. Sheep are close all around St Clement's church but a man with a power mower now controls the grass.

Orgarswick

When approximately a mile from the resort of Dymchurch and witnessing a large cross set in what appears to be a small field, anyone travelling along the Dymchurch to Bonnington road can be forgiven for assuming it is a war memorial or possibly a lonely grave. A memorial it is, but not for war victims. The cross, erected in 1932, marks the site of Orgarswick chapel, the outline foundations of which can be seen in the turf. The chapel site is a relic of distant days when this part of Romney Marsh was reclaimed, then a church or chapel built on the firm ground to serve the few souls living in the area. In the 1801 census there were six people hereabouts but presumably they gave up the struggle against harsh living and economic conditions and left, so the chapel fell into ruin. There is something rather sad when viewing such sites of which there are others on the Marsh (see *Hope All Saints* and *Eastbridge*) and it is

Cross on site of 'lost' Orgarswick church

realised that despite all these people's endeavours the hamlets only had a brief life and were unable to expand to become established villages.

Orpington

In the 19th century Orpington was a village with no particular claim to fame. In 1886 William Cook, a local resident, changed that. He introduced a breed of poultry that, through its name, the Black Orpington, was to make Orpington known throughout the poultry farming world in Britain, Europe and the Empire. More were to follow to establish Cook's reputation.

Cook began his working life at Chislehurst, probably as a coachman, but by the late 1860s he was involved in poultry farming. In 1869 he wrote his *W. Cook's Poultry Breeder & Feeder*. He was rearing poultry in 1886 while living at Tower House, Sevenoaks Road, Orpington, the property later becoming the Presbytery of Holy Innocents Roman Catholic church, now demolished. While living there he introduced and exhibited his Black Orpington, a development from the Croad Langshan, Black Minorca, Black Rock and Indian Game breeds, deciding to name it after the place where it was bred.

The Black Orpington was popular with poultry farmers, and encouraged by this in 1888 Cook introduced another new breed, the White Orpington, also successful. As his business expanded it became too large for Tower House, so he moved to Walden Manor, St Mary Cray, but renamed the property Orpington House. Here he had room for expansion, to accommodate several thousand birds, carry out research into poultry diseases and he also had a fowl hospital. He founded his own publication, *The Poultry Journal*, in 1886. It was at Orpington House that he bred the even more famous Buff Orpington which was immediately successful when exhibited in 1894. First he had mated Golden Spangled Hamburgh cocks with Coloured Dorking hens. The resulting reddish-brown pullets he then mated with a Buff Cochin cock. In 1897 Cook even introduced the Diamond Jubilee Orpington and gave several to Queen Victoria who 'was graciously pleased to accept them'.

One of his daughters, Elizabeth Jane, assisted her father in the business at Orpington House enabling Cook to introduce the Speckled Orpington hen and also the Blue and Buff Orpington ducks in 1902. William Cook died in 1904 and was interred in Star Lane cemetery, St Mary Cray, a part of the burial service taking place at Orpington Baptist church.

In 1897 one of Cook's sons, William Henry, who had also helped his father, left the business and established his own poultry farm at Elm Cottage (now Elmdene, 51 Derry Downs), St Mary Cray. On his father's death he sold his poultry farm here and established The Model Poultry Farm, St Paul's Cray, an area later known as Grays Farm. In 1911 he sold this and moved to a similar farm in Tubbenden Lane, Orpington where his business, W.H. Cook Ltd, survived until 1947 when he retired. The area became what is now Maxwell Gardens, with surrounding roads.

Elizabeth Jane continued at Orpington House after her father's death, editing *The Poultry Journal* and, in 1907, continuing her father's work, introducing the Cuckoo Orpington and Blue Orpington, managing to buy out her other brothers' and a sister's interest in the business. Another of William's sons was A. Lockley Cook and he, with his own son, established a poultry farm for egg production at Keston Court, Keston in the 1920s. The original business, William Cook and Sons, ceased in 1933 when tragically Elizabeth Jane was knocked down and killed in an accident in Bromley High Street.

Near the site of William Cook's original farm at Orpington there is a public house in Pinewood Drive now called The Buff, formerly known as The Buff Orpington. Its sign depicts the famous Buff

Orpington, keeping the name alive in the area.

Today the Orpington breeds survive as show birds. Majestic in appearance they are known as the Regal Birds, the Rolls-Royces of the Fancy. There are two enthusiastic groups, The Orpington Club and The Buff Orpington Club, dedicated to continuing the breeds. Both combined in 1986 to hold a special centenary year show of the breeds at Stafford to commemorate William Cook and his achievements with the Orpington poultry.

Otford

➤ The Green has been trespassed on by roads so that the village pond, with its weeping willows and waterfowl is now in the middle of a roundabout. Its future, however, is assured because it is the only known pond in England certified as a . . . listed building!

Patrixbourne

➤ Where in a Kent church can you see Swiss scenes in its windows? St Mary's church, Patrixbourne, and they were brought here a long time ago, the mass of enamel glass dating from 1538 to after 1670. There are 18 panels, eight in the south window of the Bifrons chapel. From the east and top to bottom they depict the Crucifixion; St John the Baptist; Pyramus and Thisbe, this panel being by Bernese workman Hans Funk; the Adoration of the Shepherds; Peter Gisler of Burglen (a town in Uri, an original canton in the Swiss Confederation. Gisler had been on a pilgrimage to Jerusalem and then was made Commissioner of Bellinzona at the entrance to the St Gothard Pass); the raising of Lazarus from the dead; a standard bearer of the Leventina valley in Tessin Canton (the winding road of the man driving pack mules being an original representation of the St Gothard Pass); the murder of St Meinrad.

In the chancel the north lancet top is Christ in Agony in the Garden of Gethsemane (the towered city in the background being Lucerne); the Crucifixion; Samson with a jawbone. The central lancet has a knight, Jacob Wirtz, 1579; a Roman soldier wearing a suit of armour resembling that made for Emperor Charles V; the Adoration of the Magi; St John the Evangelist and Elizabeth of Hungary (this being the work of Martin Moser, the top-class Lucerne glass painter in the 16th century).

The south lancet top has a painting of a long bearded knight;

Christ's Agony in the Garden of Gethsemane; Samson slaying the lion (which is an exact copy line for line of the Albrecht Dürer woodcut, the hill representing Nuremburg, Dürer's native city).

This type of glass work was often used in windows of church and other buildings in Germany and France, but it is surprising to find it in a church in the Kent countryside, and in such a complete form, although there are fragments of 17th century Swiss glass in panels in the chancel of St Peter and St Paul's church, Temple Ewell, near Dover.

Pembury

On the Green there is a memorial in the form of a horse trough. The inscription on the front states 'To the Memory of Margery Polley of Pembury who suffered martyrdom at Tonbridge AD 1555'. Another inscription reads 'Metropolitan Drinking Fountain & Cattle

The Polley memorial horse trough, Pembury

Trough Association AD 1909'. This example was 'Erected by Voluntary Subscriptions' and is now in decorative use as a plant trough.

It might be thought that the Association always paid for and provided the trough and fountain. This was so in some cases but in a considerable number local people or organisations raised the money which was then paid to the Association who supplied the trough on a site chosen and made available by a local person, organisation or authority. There were two types: one, as mentioned, in memory of someone of local or national note; two, showing kindness to animals, usually for horses, sometimes cattle, and occasionally some troughs also have a low water bowl for dogs.

In 1894 Sir David Salomons (see *Southborough*) had one placed on Southborough Common. Today, used as a flower bed, it is close to the A21; one corner is painted white to prevent vehicles colliding with it. There are Metropolitan Drinking Fountain and Cattle Trough Association troughs at Canterbury, Tunbridge Wells, Sevenoaks, Birchington and no doubt others exist. Later the RSPCA also supplied them. Other troughs are outside Sevenoaks police station and on St John's Hill, Sevenoaks. There are uninscribed examples so their source is unknown. The massive trough in Market Square, Dover, has 'Blessed Are The Merciful For They Shall Obtain Mercy' on it.

Unless they are in the way of pavement improvements or road widening, because of the size and weight of these usually granite troughs, they remain where they were originally placed.

On the Pembury to Tonbridge Road, near Fairthorne Garage, is an old wayside brick VR letter box, the bottom of the box being some 14 inches from the ground. The pillar, which the Post Office maintains, is encased on the back, sides and especially the top, with a thick mass of entwining ivy foliage, though that on the front is kept trimmed back to allow the public to post their letters. Postal history buffs may be interested to know its official description is 'Fairthorne Pembury Road, Tonbridge, the makers W.T. Allen & Co, Wall Box C, left-hand lock No. 1538090, pattern of box Pre-1905'.

Early in the 19th century a clay seam was discovered running through the Lower Green area and a brickworks was established (see *Dunton Green*) but closed at the beginning of the Second World War. In Slate Row some of the houses built for workmen still exist. Several years after the opening of the brickworks the landlord of the Royal Oak found enough clay in the public house garden to start a pottery, known as Peter's Pottery, which produced dairy pans, bread crocks, teapots, and flower pots, some of the ware being finished with a tree bark design. Tunbridge Wells Museum has examples.

Another venture at Pembury does not seem very much out of the ordinary now but the Woodsgate Road House apparently was in the 1930s, situated on the Tonbridge to Hastings road at a junction with the Tunbridge Wells Road. It was notable at that time for its swimming pool. An advertisement in the summer 1935 *Kent County Journal* stated: 'The pool is 100 ft x 40 ft with continuously *purified* and *heated* water and equipped with fixed and spring diving boards, water chutes and warm and cold showers. There are spacious terraces for sunbathing and refreshments are served at the poolside. The comfort and convenience of patrons is the first consideration, ample dressing accommodation for large numbers being provided, while a large concrete car park (free) adjoins the pool. At night the pool is illuminated by powerful floodlights. Swimming and diving lessons by an expert instructor are a speciality. Admission charges are moderate while special rates are available for regular bathers. Full particulars on request.' The advertisers claimed: 'We could say that Woodsgate Pool is the finest in the country, but you wouldn't believe it. And to be quite frank we don't say it. Nevertheless, we have hundreds of patrons who say it is the best pool they have seen. You have probably bathed in quite a few pools, but if you haven't visited Woodsgate you still have a treat in store. Why not come along and see for yourself?' After such publicity readers could hardly resist the offer unless they didn't swim!

Penshurst

At Poundsbridge hamlet, between Penshurst and Speldhurst, a mile and a half south-east of Penshurst, is a two-storeyed, half-timbered house dated 1593, known as Poundsbridge Manor, but formerly The Picture House or The Pitcher House, known by the latter name to local people. Formerly in its history it was a sort of off-licence and it is said one landlord served from a pitcher through an open window. The property was damaged by a bomb in September 1940, but was repaired post war and is now a private house.

There are two local versions on how the name Poundsbridge originated. One is that it was so named because there was a cattle pound for strays by the bridge; second, the bridge was built by a man named Pound. The 'official' version favours the latter! In 1460 it was Poundesland, seemingly 'land owned by the medieval family of Atte Punde or Atte Pound' or 'dweller by the pound'. The original bridge collapsed in a flood in 1968.

Poundsbridge Farm's garden, formerly part of the Penshurst Estate, has an ancient yellow azalea. In the 1940s it was judged to be over 100 years old, with several branches propped up. The branches have since collapsed and new growth taken over. It was thought by gardening experts that it was possibly an original import into England.

In South Park, Penshurst, stands a sweet chestnut tree claimed by experts to have been pollarded over 400 years ago. It has seven trunks above the pollard and is reputed to be the biggest tree in Europe. A pollard is a tree that has its top branches polled or cut back so that it throws out increased new growth and gains thicker wood than would be usual. In front of South Park House, bought by Sir Henry Hardinge in 1830, is a huge bronze statue of a horse and rider, designed by an Irish sculptor, J.H. Foley in 1858. The equestrian statue is of Sir Henry himself, 1st Viscount Hardinge of Penshurst, Governor-General of India 1844-48. It originally stood in The Maidan, one of Calcutta's principal streets, but when India became a republic it was removed to a municipal yard. After arrangements were made by the Hardinge family with the Indian Government in the 1960s it was removed from being under an Indian sun and re-erected here in a cooler English park.

One mile north of Penshurst, on the site of the demolished 19th century Redleaf House, some of the grounds designed by William Wells have been built on, but numerous luxurious conifers and the rockery survive, as does the original crazy paving, this being claimed to be the first place in England where crazy paving was used as part of the design.

In Coopers Lane, leading to Fordcombe, is the hamlet of Earwig Green. The postbox at the top end of the lane has the name Earwig Green and the initials GR on it. As it is known to have been in the area in 1935, formerly sited nearer the hamlet, it dates from George V's reign (see *Barming, Pembury*).

Another very interesting post box is in the sandstone wall of the Old Post Office, Penshurst. It is a wooden box with an enamel front, known as a Ludlow, having been designed by James Ludlow in 1885. Do not post any souvenir postcards in it, however, as the collection service has been withdrawn!

Petham

➤ In Town Lane, north of the main village and below the sloping Chartham arm of the North Downs, is Debden Court Farm. In 1862 Bessie Marchant,the Victorian children's novelist, was born here, into a Baptist family, and lived as a child, attending the school opposite Petham church. Eventually she taught in a Baptist school in London, married a Baptist minister and moved to Oxfordshire. She began her literary career writing moral tales for children, railing against drunkenness, extolling the soul-saving pursuit of religion and depicting the triumph of good over evil; following the same style used by children's writers of the period. Many of her early stories are set in Kent, in places she knew. *Yuppie*, 1898, is partly based on the persecution of her farmer father when at nearby Elmstead. Other villages used are given their correct names. Her characters often have the names of people she knew in her childhood. Others were taken from wall memorials in Petham church.

What set Bessie apart from other children's writers was her realisation the world was changing. The former fiction style was no longer sufficient for children who might have had fathers serving Britain and the Empire in pioneering jobs in India, Africa, and other colonies. She saw no reason why children's fiction could not relate dramatic, even taboo, subjects and events set in foreign lands. So she wrote over 150 immensely successful adventure stories for girls and died as recently as 1941.

The interior of All Saints' church is very light, especially the chancel. This is because there are only a few fragments of stained glass in the church. There was originally stained glass on the three sides of the chancel. Some time before the late 18th century the church fell on hard times and sold this glass to a private person in one instance, to Canterbury cathedral in another. Canterbury partly used it to replace windows smashed during the Commonwealth regime. Today you can see the Petham glass in the cathedral's Becket's corona and the crypt's east window.

In the old part of Petham's churchyard, surrounded by fields called Moonshine, Van Diemens Land, Long Meadow, Mill Down, close to the south chancel wall is the headstone of Thomas Crafts. His surname is underlined with an undulating serpent, a symbol of everlasting life. The date of his death, 1807, has the 7 carved upside down, as *L*. There are various beliefs about this figure. One is that the seventh son of a seventh son will always have good fortune,

Curious headstone at Petham

so it is a good symbol. It is the symbol of resurrection in the legend of the Seven Sleepers of Rome: Christian youths buried alive but brought back to life 200 years later by God. There are also the seven deadly sins, the seven sacraments, seven virtues, sometimes depicted by paintings on church walls or as carved corbels. The puzzle is why was this headstone's seven carved upside down? To show a disregard for the symbolism of seven?

Plaxtol

Between Shipbourne and Borough Green near Plaxtol the river Bourne, which supplies water for Roughway paper mill, passes the village. In the past when cottagers used whitewash and distemper for interior decoration they obtained a blue dye used in the paper production and mixed that in the whitewash. The local people called the colour 'Roughway Blue' and consequently there were numerous blue interior cottages in the area.

Pluckley

➤ Fame descended on this charming village when it became the location for much of the filming of the television adaptation of H.E. Bates' *The Darling Buds of May* (Bates lived at nearby Little Chart). Prior to this Pluckley had to live down, or live up to, its reputation as being the most ghost-ridden place in England. There was also the curious reputation of Pluckley's fair sex. A Kent saying formerly common, but hardly ever heard now, perhaps because men are more tactful to women, is 'You've got no calves to your legs like the Pluckley girls, who are obliged to wear straight stockings!' Whether there was ever any substance to this among Pluckley girls is impossible to know now and lost is the saying's origin.

The 700 year old Black Horse inn facing the Square is reputed to have one of the twelve or so ghosts in and around Pluckley. This is assumed to be responsible when objects have been mysteriously moved after human hands have definitely put them elsewhere. Perhaps it is the restless spirit of Jesse Spicer (1745-1772) who was killed in the Black Horse inn, whether by accident or deliberately is unknown. His headstone in St Nicholas churchyard, east of the church, relates ominously 'In Memory of Jesse Spicer killed by a Ninepin Bowl, aged 27'.

Queenborough

➤ In her comprehensive book *The Isle of Sheppey* Sheila Judge refers to the 1884 restoration of Holy Trinity church and what might seem a strange incident.

I quote from her account: 'The most curious story was that of the eggs. When some loose stones were removed from the south wall of the nave four hens' eggs were found in a cavity in the wall, twelve feet above ground and surrounded by masonry. The explanation for this, and it was pure conjecture, was that when the tower subsided and tipped sideways in 1630 a fissure appeared in the south wall of the nave where it joined the spiral stairway of the tower. Two strong buttresses were set against the western face of the tower to secure it and the crack was filled with masonry. This work took some time and while the fissure was still open a hen must have started a nest among the loose stones, and the workmen did not notice the eggs and so built the wall with the eggs inside. Two of the eggs were broken, the contents had shrunk and solidified, but they had retained their 'bad eggs' smell. One of the remaining eggs was kept by the mayor, the other by the vicar. The shells were rough and had become "smoky coloured" during two centuries in the wall . . .'

Of course, a hen may have come into the church and conveniently laid them, but the significance is in the four eggs. Eggs were a symbol of fertility and resurrection. They had various protective powers and like black cats, rabbits' feet, shoes, jugs, were quite commonly placed in certain parts of a building during its construction so that these 'charms' would give their benefits to it and those living in or using it. They are still occasionally found when old cottages are demolished or restored; eggs, too, but the latter more likely in a building with a religious association such as a church. Earlier generations had placed stone faces on the exterior of churches to frighten away the spirits that would cause harm; in the 17th and 18th centuries the eggs protected the actual structure. Alternatively it could be suggested a workman placed the eggs there for safe keeping for his dinner then for some reason never ate them!

An even more curious event took place in 1620 with its conclusion at Queenborough. Two men arrived in a paper boat. John Taylor, the 'Water Poet' and waterman, and Roger Bird, vintner, had accepted a wager that they could not row in such a craft from London to Queenborough. They had the frame of a rowing boat made and covered with a 'skin' of brown paper, the boat being kept afloat by eight large bladders, four on each side. Propulsion was by two 'stockfish' tied to canes (surely they cannot have been 'stockfish – cod, hake, etc, prepared for keeping by being split and dried without salt'?) On the Saturday evening tide they set off but had barely voyaged three miles when the paper bottom disintegrated. However, they paddled on, hour after hour, with only six inches of freeboard between them and sinking. Incredibly the wet and weary pair reached Queenborough on the Monday morning. Bird uttered up a prayer of thanksgiving; Taylor wrote a poem *Praise of Hempseed* about the voyage, part of it being:

'Thousands of people all the shores did hide,
And thousands more did meet us in the tide,
With scullers, oars, with ship-boats and with barges,
To gaze on us they put themselves to charges.
Thus did we drive and drive the time away,
Till pitchy night had driven away the day . . .
The tossing billows made our boat to caper,
Our paper form scarce being form of paper;
The water four miles broad, no oars to row;

Night dark and where we were we did not know;
And thus twixt doubt and fear, hope and despair,
I fell to work and Roger Bird to prayer;
And as the surges up and down did heave us,
He cried most fervently, good Lord, receive us . . .
His mercy us protected
When as we least deserved and less expected.'

Then the mayor and everyone else, it seems, in Queenborough that morning hurried to the Quay. Taylor and Bird were taken to an inn to recoup their strength with oysters and beer. The local population, seized the boat and broke it into pieces, tore off the eight bladders and the two 'stockfish' and took them home as souvenirs.

In 1667, as is well known, the Dutch invaded the Medway and caused much consternation, seizing booty and burning property. They shelled then captured Sheerness Fort, lowered the English flag and raised the Dutch. Out of this came a continuing slander concerning Queenborough. It is reputed the Dutch fired on Queenborough, ordered it to surrender or be destroyed. The mayor complied and was forced to hoist the Dutch flag from the roof of the town hall, the only time the flag of a foreign invader has been flown on a town hall in England. Research by Sheila Judge has found no evidence in English or Dutch of a mayoral surrender, a white flag or Queenborough's capture. Since 1667 at some time a 'historian' unknown has embroidered the facts to make a more interesting 'story' and the repeating by later writers has made it 'fact'.

Rainham

At the end of the 16th century, in *A Return of Shipping of Kent*, Rainham was described as having eight inhabited houses and three quays – Blowers (Bloors?), Hastings, and the 'Common' Quay. Possibly the latter may have been what was marked on maps and stated in records as the 'Parish' Wharf, at the head of Otterham Creek, for berthing craft but in more recent times used by sailing barges only in emergencies. Similarly, Lower Halstow had a 'Parish' Wharf used by sailing barges. At the time of the *Return* 13 Rainham ships and boats, from one to 35 tons, with twelve 'persons' as crews, plied from Rainham. However, Rainham did not later expand to compete as an important port rivalling Chatham, Queenborough and Sheerness. Probably water depth and continual silting by mud of

Rainham Creek deterred this, but today Bloors Wharf still exists as a commercial concern. So does nearby Otterham Quay around its Creek, where post-war development has transformed river saltings and Creek into a busy small ship and LASH (Lighter Aboard Ship) barge terminal.

I lived in Rainham as a boy and young man in the 30s and 40s when it was a large village and had not been swallowed up by Gillingham, which was expanding to earn the reputed and dubious title of being the largest borough in England, covered with the most bricks and mortar. Then Otterham Quay was lined with sailing barges. They brought in sand, river mud and 'rough stuff' or 'London Mixture' (cinders and coal ash), but if it had only been 'rough forked' before loading into the barge it was also likely to contain household refuse, vegetable matter, broken pottery, glass, even items of value sometimes, trinkets, etc. The 'rough stuff' was heaped in huge mounds adjacent to the Windmill Hill sand-cliff and the Quay Lane brick fields near where a post war housing estate was built on Banky Field. The mounds sometimes remained for up to a year to allow vegetation content to rot before the 'rough stuff' was sifted and used with mud, sand, clay, sometimes chalk, to make bricks at Eastwoods brickworks. The bricks were loaded on to their own barges and transported to London, or if to inland destinations taken by lorry.

The Romans had come this way when constructing their Watling Street, the A2, over 'Rainham Downs' en route to London. They drained some of the northern marshes, established extensive potteries close to Upchurch and built villas, one site being near Hartlip. On a map of Rainham it will be noticed there are several parallel thoroughfares leading from Watling Street to the Lower Rainham road, creeks and marshes, such as Pump Lane, Bloors Lane, Berengrave Lane, Quay Lane and others. This is no coincidence. The Lower Rainham Road is an ancient British trackway, which was in existence before the Romans arrived and linked it to their Watling Street. These routes divided the land into more or less parallel strips or squares. It was the Roman practice in conquered regions to provide land for retired army veterans who decided to settle there. A 'private' was usually granted 25 to 30 acres, an 'NCO' twice this acreage. A yoke of oxen was also given to each man, with enough seed to establish himself as a smallholder. These men are not thought to have lived separately on their valuable land, but as a community in a settlement built for or by them, on this occasion on or near Motney Hill. A Roman cemetery has been discovered as evidence and is still visible, though overgrown, north of the Lower Rainham Road and east of the former Goldsmiths cement works site.

Following more recently in the footsteps of the Romans the Baker family revived local pottery by establishing a works near Upchurch prior to the First World War. A heavy type of glazed pottery of varied smoky patterns or plain colour was produced. Another pottery was established just before the Second World War near the Men of Kent Inn, Rainham, producing varied ware. Both have closed, Rainham Pottery in 1975, but the products of each are now keenly sought by collectors of former Kent pottery wares.

There was great excitement in Rainham in February 1868. An underground gas supply to all the roads and streets in the then village was finished. The gas lamp standards awaited erection while the Rochester Gas company officials and local dignitaries proudly celebrated with a dinner and speeches at the old White Horse Inn, High Street. The *Chatham News* reported: 'The front of the inn was illuminated with a large gaslit "star", which was the source of great attraction during the evening. The old church, on the opposite side of the street, was also seen to great advantage from the glare of the light thrown upon it'. The Band of the 16th Kent Rifles arrived. They set up their music-stands in front of the church and made history as 'they gave Rainham its first open-air, after-dark recital of music'.

Earlier generations of Rainham men would not have welcomed this illumination of the are at night. The customary yew, now venerable and showing its age, overlooked the scene from St Margaret's churchyard. As well as guarding the souls of the dead it then also sometimes guarded the souls of the living. In the days of press gangs from Chatham seizing victims, when a warning arrived in Rainham that such a gang was coming any eligible men in the street who were unable to flee hid in the yew's abundant green foliage until danger had literally passed by.

Ramsgate

◥ Between Ramsgate and Dumpton Bay, at East Cliff, is the 13-acre King George VI Memorial Park. Here formerly stood East Cliff Lodge, built between 1794 and 1799, the main house being demolished in 1954. All that survives are some high flint walls that surrounded it, the gatekeeper's lodge and stables, and an early 19th century, lean-to Italianate conservatory, against a 15 ft high crenallated, late 18th century outer brick wall. One of the early owners of East Cliff Lodge was Admiral Lord George Keith, Commander of the Channel Squadron, as he was able to get a good view of the squadron from his home. The then Princess of Wales, later Queen Caroline, was a frequent visitor. It was said she liked grapes so much Admiral Keith decided to grow them specially for her. In 1805 he had the conservatory built and the vine inside it imported from Corsica.

From 1822 to 1885 the Lodge was the home of Sir Moses Montefiore, a Victorian philanthropist, who stocked the conservatory with tropical plants and shrubs. The conservatory is believed to be in a style of which there are only three others of similar design in Britain. It has a panelled base wall with long supports on internal cast iron columns. As the conservatory swells outwards to base level the curing cast iron frame structure has painted copper glazing bars containing 9,000 panes of unusual scalloped-edge glass that also curve and overlap like fish scales. There are central, double, half-glazed entrance doors under a pediment with scrolled tracery, the interior not only preserving the original structure but also the benches, supports and heating system.

In the 1960s, due to changes in local administration, the conservatory was neglected and vandalised. There was a possibility of its demolition, but the Ramsgate Society and others fought for its restoration, raising funds to achieve this. The glass was removed for cleaning and replacement where cracked or missing, then the structure was taken to the workshop of a local firm, W.W. Bishop. Their craftsmen spent seven months repairing and welding the iron frame. It was put together again and when complete reconstructed in its original position.

From this park there is a pleasant walk from the East Cliff in a south-westwards direction to inner Ramsgate, passing the Victoria Gardens, with 'Pulhamite' rocks, opened in 1892, and after passing the stately Wellington Crescent proceeding downhill into the interesting Madeira Walk. This was created in 1893 as a result of developments linking the East and West Cliffs, also being constructed by the London company, Pulham, who built Folkestone's Zig-Zag Path. Using large specimens of their rather flattish square and oblong artificial rock boulders, made by their 'Pulhamite' process, the company deliberately arranged these to have the appearance of a rocky ravine. A wood rustic bridge spanned across the top from which passers-by could view the impressive cascade or waterfall flowing below, various plants and shrubs being planted to heighten the effect. On special occasions the area's beauty was enhanced with the waterfall being illuminated during darkness by revolving lamps of various colours or by thousands of fairy lights glittering along the rocky slopes. In the driest of long ago summers it did not stop running and was only officially discontinued for maintenance. I can remember it flowing within the last 20 years, but regrettably no longer does this to provide a spectacular tourist attraction.

On No. 6, Royal Road a plaque states 'Painter Vincent van Gogh taught here in 1876'. Difficult to believe but true. Aged 23 he arrived in Ramsgate from Holland on a month's trial in April 1876, to take up an unpaid teaching job, board and lodging only, for a Methodist minister, Revd William Stokes, who ran a private school for boys at Royal Road. The latter forms a terrace of several-storey houses, part of Spencer Square on West Cliff, the artist with some of the boys sleeping at 11 Spencer Square. While teaching here van Gogh, full of enthusiasm for the area, sent home sketches of Ramsgate and Pegwell Bay, both views and properties. One was the Paragon Corner House, now the Churchill Tavern. Two months after the artist's arrival in Ramsgate Revd Stokes moved the school to Isleworth and van Gogh went with him, even being paid a small wage, but eventually he returned to Holland and, as they say, the rest is history.

Reculver

Between Birchington and Herne Bay on the north Kent coast at a site where the Romans in the third century AD built a fort, Regulbium, to defend the northern entrance to the Wantsum Channel, stand the two towers of the demolished St Mary's church, 'Our Lady of Reculver'. The towers, maintained by Trinity House to preserve them as a seamark for seafarers, each formerly had a spire and are still known as the 'Two Sisters'. There is a legend behind this name, which says that in the 15th century there were two orphaned daughters of Sir Geoffrey St Clare, Frances and Isabella. Frances took the veil and became Abbess of Faversham. Isabella, under the guardianship of John, Abbot of Canterbury, was betrothed to Henry de Belville, who fought for Richard III and was fatally injured at the Battle of Bosworth Field.

Isabella then also took the veil, living with her sister for 14 years until Frances was taken ill with fever. The sisters vowed that if Frances recovered they would go on a pilgrimage and make offerings at the Shrine of St Mary, Bradstowe (Broadstairs). Frances did recover and they set out by ship from Faversham to fulfil their vows, but off Reculver the ship was driven on to a sandbank. Frances was rescued by some seafarers but Isabella had to stay on the wreck until it got light when she was brought ashore only to die from exposure in her sister's arms. Frances alone completed the pilgrimage to Bradstowe on foot, then in her sister's memory she restored the church and erected the two spires on the towers, known afterwards as the 'Two Sisters'. The puzzle is why undertake the journey by sea in the first place when they could easily and safely have made the short distance from Faversham to Bradstowe by land on foot in a day?

The Saxon church was built on the site of the Roman fort about 669, the foundations of it, using Roman materials, being discovered during excavations in 1927. The church was enlarged in the eighth, twelfth, thirteenth and fifteenth centuries. The two towers being built during the twelfth. The leaded wooden spires were still in position in 1876, but some time after that were removed.

Excavations have been done periodically on the square fort, with its ten ft thick walls, revealing several periods of Roman road building, the main road within the fort running from east to west, with remains of a headquarters building and officers' houses immediately south of it. Traces of a civil settlement outside the fort have been recorded on three sides, but no doubt there is much more hidden and awaiting revelation, especially wharves and other constructions along the line of the Wantsum Channel to Richborough, and who knows what is in the silted Wantsum bed itself.

There is also a local legend that on a dark night the cries of babies can be heard by anyone standing among the ruins of the Roman fort. Unbelievers have dismissed it as a superstitious nonsense . . . until excavations by the Kent Archaeological Unit uncovered a basis for the legend. In 1966 the unit excavated a Roman barrack block on the west side of the fort, built about AD 200-250.

Two small sections of the wall of the building were removed to allow examination of the wall's construction.

To the surprise of the unit's archaeologists the skeleton of a young infant was found beneath the first wall section. Then beneath the second section of the wall two more infant skeletons were discovered. It is certain these infants were deliberately placed in this position by the builders of the Roman barracks and are regarded as foundation burials, the purpose of which was probably to give the building a 'soul' or to placate the gods and protect the building. There was no evidence to indicate the infants had been sacrificed and they almost certainly died a natural death. The Romans were also known to use stillborn babies for this purpose. In later centuries black cats and various other objects were put in the walls of new cottages to satisfy rural superstition (see *Queenborough*).

But how did the 'crying babies' legend start? Did someone really hear them? More likely as the sea eroded away the walls of the former Roman buildings on the site other infant skeletons were seen in the same position and thus from their sighting arose this legend.

Rochester

There has been conjecture as to where Charles Dickens obtained the names of his characters. Some are obviously those of relatives, friends and acquaintances with a simple adaptation, others he noted down when seen, as all story writers do, in case they come in useful. He often attended at Rochester cathedral and visited the city. He frequently thus passed by the graveyard alongside the cathedral. A particular headstone a few feet from the pavement would not have been missed as he walked by. The deceased commemorated are still: John Dorrett, died October 1837, aged 52; Rebecca Dorrett, died September 1839, aged 59 years; Fanny Dorrett died August 1851, aged 79 years. Written and published in 1856 could these be the inspiration for *Little Dorrit*?

Across the road from the cathedral's west front is the small burial ground where Dickens hoped to be interred. If he had he would no doubt have been quite as content lying opposite the Dorrett family and among those people he knew and described so skilfully – Benjamin Bassett, Ann Young, William Say, James Brown and other Rochester citizens therein – as among the illustrious in Westminster Abbey. The Abbey is more worthy of him as the burial ground he favoured is now an island bounded by a busy road. But he almost was interred in Rochester cathedral.

The *Chatham News* of June 1870 stated regarding a site for Dickens' interment: 'It was reported that the deceased had expressed a wish to be buried in that part of the St Nicholas' burial ground, Rochester, immediately beneath Rochester Castle Wall. The request was made to the Home Secretary for the burial ground to be opened to receive the body of Mr Dickens but a refusal was made on the grounds that Mr Dickens did not live within the parish of St Nicholas'. The newspaper reported that a request had been made to inter Dickens at Cobham churchyard, but this was again refused as the churchyard was almost full and the parish council wanted the land remaining to be for their own dead, Dickens not being a local resident.

Seeing an opportunity in a situation where no one seemed to want to have the grave of Dickens, the Dean and Chapter of Rochester cathedral employed 'a strong party of workmen to execute the work' and dig a grave in St Mary's Chapel, Rochester cathedral, at the east end of the nave and a vault formed 'for the reception of the remains of the illustrious dead'. But while they were still preparing this vault it was decided to inter him in Westminster Abbey and, says the *Chatham News*, 'the grave was prepared in great secrecy. Early on Tuesday morning the body was removed in a hearse from Gad's Hill Place to Higham Station for conveyance to London by special train which also carried mourners. This train left Higham at 8 o'clock and very few people knew about it. From Charing Cross terminus the coffin was removed from the train to a plain hearse and taken to Westminster Abbey. The funeral took place at 9.30, only close relatives being admitted to the funeral. The grave is situated at the foot of the coffin of Handel and at the head of the coffin of Sheridan. The grave was left open all day and thousands of people filed past it.' Meanwhile, back at Rochester cathedral on the same morning the vault was filled up with the earth taken from digging the grave and the paving restored so there was little indication of where Dickens' grave could have been, 'the bell of the cathedral tolling for the funeral of the dead Dickens [in London] while the workmen were refilling the vault [at Rochester]'.

In the High Street, behind the red-brick Tudor Eastgate House, is a small public garden, pleasant with a fountain and goldfish ponds. On one side is the Swiss chalet from Gad's Hill given to Dickens by his actor friend, Charles Fechter, in which he often worked on his novels. It was acquired by Rochester City Council in 1961, fully restored and re-erected here. Nearby is another item from Dickens' home at Gad's Hill, the horse powered pump with its large iron wheel, installed there by Dickens in 1857 to raise water from a well for the household. It was brought from Gad's Hill and placed on its present site for preservation in 1973.

Adjoining it is something else brought here to protect it, a section of medieval road. It was part of the approach road to the 1387 Rochester Bridge being excavated at Strood in 1897. It is similar to cobblestones and one of the ruts made in it by the transport of the time can be seen.

Leaning over the Esplanade's balustrade as the wide Medway flows past and now much cleaner, it is not difficult to realise why the Mayor and Corporation have had age-old rights over the 'floating fish', an archaic term for the river's marine inhabitants which even included oysters and other shellfish. In centuries past these are known from records to have been profusely abundant. As far back as Edward IV a charter was granted to the Mayor and 'citizens' entitling them to 'all fishes to be caught within the liberty and precincts of the city and belonging to us and our heirs'. This included the royal fish, the sturgeon. In July, 1630, a sturgeon was caught by one John Porritt and taken to the Mayor and 'eaten by him and his brethren'. In the 19th century two more were caught. One was presented to the Archbishop of Canterbury and its fate is unknown. In the 1870s the other, weighing about 100 lbs, 6 ft 9 inches long, was caught by a Strood fisherman with hook and line in the Medway here. It took him and his son over an hour to land it. On doing so he presented it to Rochester's Mayor and Corporation, but they put it in a box with ice, a very long box, too, and a corporation official delivered it personally to Windsor Castle, Queen Victoria apparently having been graciously pleased to accept it.

Rolvenden

➤ South-east of the village is Great Maytham Hall, a mansion built 1909-1910, designed in neo-Georgian style by Sir Edwin Lutyens, the centre block incorporating part of a smaller house of 1721, Lutyens adding above and around it. It has a significance in literary history. From 1898 to 1907 it was leased by the novelist and dramatist Frances Hodgson Burnett. She was born in Manchester, and after a Lancashire childhood, during which she found an abandoned garden in Salford, she went with her parents to the USA in 1865 and married a Dr Burnett in 1873. She began to publish novels in 1867 but it was not until 1886 that *Little Lord Fauntleroy* made her a best selling author.

Burnett was an enthusiastic gardener, her last book being *In the Garden*, about her thoughts and experiences. Back in England it was the 'beautiful old walled kitchen garden' at Great Maytham Hall that attracted her although it was an old orchard that had become overgrown through dereliction. She wrote to her son in America: 'It was entered by a low, arched gateway in the wall, closed by a wooden door. The ground underneath the twisted, leaning old apple trees was cleared of all its weeds and thorns and sown with grass and then, at every available place, roses were planted to climb up the ancient trunks and over the walls.' Here were the original of the rose garden, the robin and the lamb she used in her book *The Secret Garden*, published in 1911. She planned this at Great Maytham Hall but wrote it at Plandome, Long Island, after returning to the USA in 1907. She first called it *Mistress Mary* when writing it in 1910 but later changed this to the title familiar to us. Even so, the book did not then have the popularity of *Little Lord Fauntleroy* and when she died in 1924 *The Times* did not even mention it in her obituary. Since then it has steadily grown in popularity after reprinting regularly, also having been made into a children's TV film, a cinema film and a musical, but in Britain Frances Hodgson Burnett herself is still virtually unknown as its author.

Today Great Maytham Hall is divided into flats run by the Country Houses Association, but the garden's high walls survive, the gardens being open to the public on Wednesday and Thursday afternoons from May to September.

In St Mary the Virgin's church is a commemorative tablet, made by Tiffany's of New York, which relates Rolvenden's link with this author and her classic books. There is also a memorial to Lt. Henry Tennant, RFC, from Great Maytham Hall, who was killed during the First World War, designed by Sir Edwin Lutyens and situated above the north chapel door.

St Mary-in-the-Marsh

St Mary the Virgin is another church with a story behind its clock. A Turkish bey ordered it from Benson's, clockmakers, just prior to the First World War. The war began in 1914, and as Turkey was then Britain's enemy the clock was not delivered to its would-be customer. Presumably it languished with its maker until, the war over, St Mary's wanted something useful as a war memorial, so the parish council bought and erected the Turkish bey's clock.

Some time since the 1960s another memorial I remember has vanished. On the north and east walls of the chancel by the altar there were unusual colour paintings, of Christ, St Paul, and Moses, painted on what appeared to be linoleum or canvas-type material with oil paints, these dedicated in memory of the children and brother of a past rector, Revd E.W. Woollatt, incumbent from 1901-1915. These paintings have disappeared from the walls, but what has appeared, though on the south-west wall by the door, is a painted and gilded scene that looks like a replica medieval altarpiece, possibly part of a triptych, with carved wood religious figures. Has the latter been introduced to replace the former for some reason? It has to be admitted their removal does make the chancel more light and airy.

In the porch the two benches adjacent to the walls were used for the first school here, the priest acting as schoolteacher (see *Chilham*).

St Nicholas-at-Wade

Within churches, ledger stones and brasses in the floor indicate the deceased were interred thereunder. Some may have been notable or landed, or nobodies who just had the money to buy themselves a resting place inside the church in the dry. The more they paid the closer they got to the side altars or the chancel altar. St Nicholas has a number of ledger stones but it was where there are none that proved of considerable interest in January 1983. Then a man using a ladder in the centre aisle to replace light bulbs felt some of the tiled floor sink under the weight. A hole appeared which, on being widened after the vicar was summoned, exposed a chamber containing human bones. Some of the skeletons were still among the crumbling remains of wood coffins, others without coffins were among remnants of their shrouds. It was an interior burial place, not uncommon (see *Upchurch*), except it seems to have been unmarked unless the tiles covered these details.

What was unusual, however, was that one skeleton had been positioned to face the other skeletons. It was surmised this was a priest who had been interred in this position so that on the Day of Judgement he would be facing his congregation. The bones, which were estimated to be from between 15 to 20 bodies and several hundred years old, were removed. After examination of the eight ft deep burial chamber it was filled in and the bones re-interred. A six inch concrete slab was placed over the site and the area retiled with tiles that approximately match the originals.

Sandhurst

➤ Sandhurst parish is sited just inside the county's south-west boundary, adjoining the Kent Ditch, a natural feature improved by man, which here separates Kent from Sussex and its Weald. St Nicholas church, a mile from Sandhurst village, overlooks the Ditch and Bodiam Castle below. It has been claimed, and there is no reason to dispute it, that Sandhurst's massive sandstone 14th century tower was used in troubled times by the castle's occupants as a look-out post. No doubt if they had seen anything amiss from it they would have dashed back into Sussex and the castle to hurriedly close and bar the gates.

In the churchyard at rest are two people who, in their quite different ways, benefited other people's lives. Dr Vincent Nesfield, FRCS (1879-1972) was an outstanding doctor and surgeon and on reading his life story obviously a man ahead of his time. As a young man, a doctor with the Indian Medical Service, he saw the results of sour, impure drinking water. It was his pioneering work on its purification by chlorine that led to water sterilisation, of immense benefit to mankind. Dr Nesfield a local GP, who ran a nursing home at Sandhurst and had a Harley Street practice, was also a specialist in the treatment of some forms of cancer, back and eye problems. During the Second World War the actor Esmond Knight suffered severe eye injuries while serving in the Royal Navy. London eye specialists said that nothing could be done for his 'blindness'. Dr Nesfield treated him and eventually Knight recovered enough sight to allow him to continue acting. Several years later a grateful patient cured of cancer paid for a new lifeboat at Eastbourne, named *Vincent Nesfield* by Esmond Knight.

The other resident referred to was 'Patience Strong', the poet and author, whose own name was Winifred Cushing, née May. Her vast output of poems in magazines and books, in particular her 'Quiet Corner', can rightly be said to have raised the daily morale of her immense reading public, many of whom no doubt would never have otherwise read poetry. Her own life, however, was tinged with sad events. Her first husband, Frederick Williams, died as a result of an accident; her second husband, Sherlock (Guy) Cushing, from lung cancer. She had an aunt in Eastbourne and through visiting her 'Patience Strong' came to know the Kent-Sussex border area well. Firstly, she lived near Battle, Sussex, and then, according to her autobiography she moved to properties, Southways and Meadow Cottage, in the Sandhurst area which must have given her so much inspiration for her work. She later returned to Sussex, at Sedlescombe, but on her death in 1990 she was interred with her first husband, Frederick Williams, at Sandhurst, her second husband having been cremated. Her funeral was attended by a large number of the public.

Sandwich

Despite what Hubert de Burgh boasted regarding Dover while Constable of Dover Castle between 1203 and 1215: 'Never as long as I draw breath will I resign to French aliens this castle which is the very key and gate of England', in reality, between the 11th and 13th centuries when it was at the height of its busy importance because of the shelter of its then deep-water Haven, the 'gateway of England' was . . . Sandwich. To and fro came and went kings and queens, noblemen, statesmen, merchants, pilgrims. Spices, leather goods, silks and other 'cloths', wines, glass and other ware arrived. These rich pickings attracted frequent raids from the French to plunder the town. The mayors of Sandwich wear black gowns in memory of Mayor John Drury and other citizens murdered by the French in 1457. I would like to have been there to see the effect on local people who in 1255 witnessed at The Quay at Sandwich the arrival of the first elephant to come to England. It was a gift from the King of France to our Henry III for the latter's zoo in the Tower of London. Presumably they had their own reasons why they landed it here to walk to London instead of delivering it to the Tower's own quay. Passing through Wingham near Canterbury the elephant saw a bull in a field and stopped. The bull became enraged and charged the elephant. The latter merely used its trunk and tusks to stop the bull, heave it into the air and crash it to the ground with such an impact the bull was killed.

Sandwich can also claim another first. In 1560 Queen Elizabeth I granted permission for the Flemings to live in the town. They arrived in considerable numbers to escape from Spanish persecution in the Netherlands. Among the various crafts and other means of earning a living that they brought was market gardening. It was these refugees who grew the first celery in England at Sandwich in 1561. Some of the land around Sandwich is still called by the Flemish name of 'polders' or 'poulders', there being a Great Poulders Farm between Sandwich and Woodnesborough.

In 1573 Queen Elizabeth herself visited Sandwich and stayed at what is now the 'King's Lodging' for three days. She was royally entertained with 'a banket of 160 dishes on a table 28 feet long in the scole house (now Manwood Court) . . . wheare she was very merrye and did eate of dyvers dishes . . .' As part of the festivity she watched the sport of boat tilting. In this two boats, presumably the rowing boat type, took part, one man in each, with a cross plank linking the two craft. Then each man stood up, got on the plank armed with a staff and holding a wooden shield. They tilted at each other as the boats rocked about until one of the two men overbalanced, or was pushed, and fell in the water to the amusement of those watching.

A second version is that there were two men in each rowing boat, the oarsman to provide motive power, the other to joust with the 'enemy'. The seated oarsman rowed at the 'enemy' and kept the boat positioned while his 'tiltsman' standing on a plank in the bows and using his staff attempted in a sort of waterborne jousting tournament to force the 'enemy' off his plank in the rival boat.

St Bartholomew's 'hospital' at the Deal/Dover end of New Street is believed by some sources to have been founded in 1217 as a thanksgiving for a resounding defeat of the French by the Sandwich Fleet on St Bartholomew's Day 1217, although as far earlier as 1190 food and shelter were provided here for pilgrims and travellers en route to Canterbury. Another possibility is that by an edict of Pope Innocent IV it was founded by Sir Henry de Sandwich in 1244. It was about 1300 that the premises became a resident hospital for townsfolk only. Today the 13th century chapel which survives is surrounded by a quadrangle of mainly Victorian almshouses.

St Bartholomew's Day is 24th August. In the past, through part of the town a procession was held, comprising the Sandwich laity, some using musical instruments, others bearing wax candles, followed by the clergy singing or chanting hymns and carrying tapers, these being followed by the higher ranks of local citizens. Today the procession is still held, but is much shorter, only being from the Master of the Hospital's House to the chapel. After this ceremony the children of the town taking part have to run around the chapel. Perhaps this is to impress upon them the custom to ensure they continue it when they are adults, a practice with customs elsewhere, such as 'beating the bounds'. Then each child receives a reward, a 'Bartlemas bun', more a biscuit, on which the image of the saint and the wording 'Founded AD 1190 Sandwich' is impressed.

Sevenoaks

At the north end of the town is The Vine, reputed to be the oldest cricket ground in England, though Bearsted and others may dispute this. Triangular in shape it was given to Sevenoaks in 1773 by the playing cricket-lover John, 3rd Duke of Dorset, of Knole House. Though the game had been played here earlier, the first nationally reported cricket match took place in 1734 when Kent defeated Sussex. In 1902 seven oak trees were planted beside the ground to commemorate the coronation of Edward VII. Six of them were destroyed by the hurricane in October 1987, but replacements have been planted so the town can still live up to its name. In the 1950s seven young oak trees were also planted on the southern edge of the town, in a row on the west side of the Tonbridge road, south of the White Hart inn, having now grown to some 30 ft high. This would indicate there are really 14 oaks at Sevenoaks.

It is to be wondered why on the wooded greensand ridge, when oaks were common, the number seven was used. Why not six oaks or eight oaks? It may be there was a group of seven oaks that Saxon settlers used as their meeting place. Here again comes to notice the figure seven (see *Petham*). Even William Lambarde, author of *A Perambulation of Kent*, 1575, was uncertain, referring to it by its ancient name 'Sennocke, or, as some call it, Seven oke, of a number of trees as they conjecture . . .' Hasted referred to them as seven 'large' trees which stood on the hill 'at the time of the first building'. As Dorothy Gardiner suggests in her *Companion into Kent*, 1934, 'After all, the name might well commemorate seven mighty trees felled to provide beams for the first Saxon settlers on the spot . . .'

Entering Knole Park, via the main entrance opposite St Nicholas church in Tonbridge Road, a steep hill descends into a valley that was formerly the bed of a vanished river flowing into the Darenth. Opposite is Ice-House Hill and from the footpath towards the summit of the hill the mound of the ice-house is visible, used to preserve food for summer use. In a hollow is the small Bird House, a sort of useful folly, built in a pseudo-Gothic style probably to house Lord Amherst's collection of exotic birds, though it has since been occupied by humans. Lord Amherst had been Ambassador in China and returned home with these birds, among them a pheasant, *Phasianus Amherstiae*. There was a small interior court at Knole called the Pheasant Court as he kept some of these pheasants there. The flint and rubble sham ruins near the Bird House (see *Sheerness, Dover*) were built about 1761 when such follies were in vogue. Vita

Sackville-West said of the Bird House that she was frightened by it when a child and thought it was like the witch's house in *Hansel and Gretel*, tucked away in its hollow.

She also stated that Knole House has 'seven courtyards to correspond to the days of the week, its fifty-two staircases to the weeks of the year, its three hundred and sixty-five rooms to the days of the year.'

Jane Austen was also a visitor to Sevenoaks. She often visited her great-uncle, Francis Austen, a solicitor with offices in the northern end of the High Street. He lived in the late 17th century red-brick Red House, also in the High Street, opposite the early 19th century White House. In July 1788, when she was twelve years old Jane herself lived for a while with her great-uncle at the Red House. He died in 1791 aged 92 and left it in his will to his son Francis Motley Austen, who owned it until 1796 when he sold it to purchase Kippington House in Kippington Road. On Francis' death in 1815 Kippington House passed to his son, Colonel Thomas Austen. The latter was involved in a dispute with the Sevenoaks populace in 1820. When Queen Caroline, whose treatment by George IV earned her much public sympathy, refused to accept the annuity her husband offered her to leave the country, rejoicing took place in Sevenoaks as elsewhere, but Colonel Austen refused to join in this, so the irate population marched to Kippington House and smashed all its windows.

Hugh Wyatt Standen in his thoroughly researched *Kippington in Kent*, privately published in 1958, endeavoured to find any surviving Austen connection with Sevenoaks. I quote: '. . . I have only been able to trace one piece of evidence connecting the old family name of Austen with Sevenoaks today and that is in the little antique brass plate (2¼ inches by 4 inches) inscribed THE BOUNDARY OF MRS AUSTEN'S LAND 1728 dug up recently at the boundary separating the grounds of The Old House in the High Street, where Mrs Austen was living, from those of the Red House, where Dr Fuller was living. The plate is now fixed to the brick wall adjoining the front door of the house which Miss Joan Constant built in the grounds of The Red House about six years ago and which she has named "Austens".'

Shadoxhurst

A church clock has a public face, the reason for its being, but the mechanism is hidden within the tower or turret and only seen by the person who regularly climbs to wind it, unless it is now electrically driven. At St Peter and St Paul church, Shadoxhurst, this does not entirely apply. After a public subscription raised the sum needed the clock was built in 1920 by H.M. Hartley of Shillingford and put in position as a memorial to those who died in the 1914-18 war and as a thanksgiving for those men and women of the parish who returned safely, being dedicated in 1921. The clock's single face as usual tells the time, situated in the small, square, oak shingle roofed, one-bell turret at the west end of the church; but its weight-driven mechanism and heavy pendulum are far from hidden. They are exposed to view – and hearing – at pew level in the nave, but now enclosed in a glass case to protect them from dust and probably human interference. The clock's hands are operated by a long shaft with one-to-twelve reduction gears in the turret. The weights have to be wound up twice a week.

Local historian L.M. Chowns, in his excellent privately published *Shadoxhurst, A Village History*, 1977, relates: 'In 1963 birds built a nest in these gears and I climbed up through the trap door and cleared this and restarted the mechanism. In 1965 a weight-cable broke, fortunately while the weight was near the floor . . . On one occasion, in the 1930s, a cable snapped when the driving weight was near the top of its travel and the cast iron ring weights crashed down on to the framing supporting the clock. The whole of the mechanism hung drunkenly from the wall. Hurried work by Mr Alec Bingham and his men from the wheelwright's shop was necessary to put things right.' Even church clocks it seems have their ups and downs.

The weather vane on the 1869 turret, like the clock, is also unusual if not unique. It is shaped like a large human hand in a gauntlet. As the turret has been replaced several times so the weather vane has been transferred from the old to the latest turret.

Sheerness

The folly of Sheerness is a sight that is far from hidden, though some residents and even visitors have outspokenly said it ought to be, but whatever a person's view this 'structure' is a part of the history of Sheerness.

In 1858 a sailing ship, the *Lucky Escape,* ran aground here. She was carrying a cargo of cement in barrels. One version is that several days after the shipwreck her cargo floated ashore. The second version is the cargo was unloaded on the beach but got soaked by a tide, with the same outcome. Whichever is true the cement in the barrels got wet and either way an unnamed but enterprising farmer is said to have salvaged the barrels. The cement in them eventually dried out and hardened, so the farmer broke off the staves and used the barrel-shaped upright cement blocks to build the grotto-like folly walls, also including flints and any rubble that was handy. The shape of the barrels can be seen today in the folly alongside the Ship on Shore inn, on Marine Parade, Sheerness, the inn having a depiction of the *Lucky Escape* ashore on its sign.

The mystery, however, is where did the cement come from? Just along the coast at Queenborough Creek, south of Sheerness, Sheppey had its own source of cement; Castle's Cement Works, that survived until 1912. Could the *Lucky Escape* have been carrying Queenborough cement when she ran aground and the folly blocks originated a mere two miles away?

Folly 'ship on shore', Sheerness

In June 1756, something else useful to the residents was driven ashore near here. It was 'a monstrous fish', almost certainly a whale, 36 ft long, 22 ft in circumference, eight ft from the eyes to the tip of its 'nose'. It yielded 20 hogsheads of oil which the residents would have used for lighting and heating.

Shepherdswell

The village of Shepherdswell has the rare distinction of two railway stations. One is the British Rail station en route to and from Dover. The second is hidden behind a screen of trees about 200 yards away. This is the terminus of the East Kent Light Railway. The latter was constructed between 1911 and 1917 to serve the growing number of coal mines being sunk in East Kent. The consortium of mine and land owners envisaged a line that would link the collieries with the main line route and a new port at Richborough. In fact, Richborough became an important port during the First World War, but the railway line did not cross the river Stour until after the war, by which time the port was in decline. Branches to Canterbury, Deal and Birchington had also been planned. Work started on a Canterbury extension but it was never completed, nor were the other lines built. The line that was constructed was to the standard gauge of 4 ft 8.5 inches, laid to light railway standards by the well-known engineer, Col. H.F. Stephens. Passengers were first carried in 1916 although few facilities were provided for them and traffic dwindled.

With the collapse of the various coal mining ventures the railway was starved of revenue and this led to part of the route's closure following nationalisation in 1948. Only one section, from Shepherdswell to Tilmanstone Colliery, was kept open for traffic, until the miners' strike of 1984. Although the colliery reopened for a short time after the strike it was eventually closed in 1986. Official closure of the line by British Rail followed in 1987.

The track was not lifted, however, because in 1985 the East Kent Light Railway Society had been formed with the aim of purchasing the line as a working museum railway and again carrying passengers over what was left of the East Kent Light Railway. It was not until 1989 that Society members first moved on to the former Shepherdswell (EKLR) station site after leasing it from British Rail, to begin the massive task of clearing the tangle of trees, bushes, bramble and weeds that had grown since the coal trains had been withdrawn. Following that time the entirely volunteer workforce has reconstructed the platform and associated buildings, provided toilets, car parks and access roadways to enable visitors to enjoy their visit to the railway with a railway buffet inside a historic coach, there also being a miniature railway for children to ride behind a small-scale steam engine. The track has been restored, along with the other stations on the line, and the East Kent Light Railway is now a thriving passenger-carrying railway.

In the meantime, the Society has a collection of interesting locomotives, coaches and other rolling stock available for viewing by the public. On the site there is the East Kent Railway Museum with many items linked to the line. The site is open throughout the year for visitors to see the completed work. Special event days are arranged during the main operating period of Easter to Christmas, which include an annual 'Steam Up', a miniature railway weekend, and 'Mince Pie Specials'. All this taking place behind a screen of trees on what is almost a hidden, secret railway.

Shipbourne

The name, from Olde English *scir burn*, means 'bright or clear stream'. In 1226 it had evolved to Sibburn; in 1292 was Shipburne, but late in the 13th century the name seems to have been revised to give the meaning of 'sheep stream'. In the Kent dialect 'sheep' was pronounced 'ship', as it must have been in Shakespeare's county, for in his *Two Gentlemen of Verona*, Act 1, Scene 1 he writes: 'Twenty to one, then, he is shipp'd already, And I have played the sheep [pronounced ship] in loving him.' There is a stream on the edge of the village that used to have a bay, a dam built in ditches to retain water, and here sheep used to be washed before shearing.

In the parkland of nearby Fairlawne estate is a large sprint, the Lady Vane Spring (the Vanes having been a local family involved with Charles I and II and Cromwell) that rises from 1,200 ft down in the Hythe Beds, geologically calcareous sandstone.

On one side of the village green is a property of national importance (see *Kingsgate*) called The Wood House. Its construction was commissioned by Jack Donaldson, then assisting in running a new pioneer health centre in Peckham, and his wife Frances, daughter of Frederick Lonsdale, the playwright, herself an author and biographer, having had much success with her biography *Edward VIII*. The Wood House was designed by Walter Gropious in 1937, one of only two commissions he undertook in England before leaving for the USA, taking the style with him. He left before the house was finished, to be completed by his partner Maxwell Fry. Its significance is that in this period when white reinforced concrete was in vogue for modern style houses Gropius returned to using a previous age's style and faced the house with creosoted wooden weatherboarding – overlapping horizontal boards usually covering and protecting from rain a timber-framed wall, hence its name. Later Frances Donaldson commented on the house: 'This creation was not much admired by the English, who dislike modern architecture too much to know the difference between good and bad, but it has been listed as Grade Two and is often visited by foreigners'.

Sholden

Opposite St Nicholas church is Sholden Hall, a Georgian mansion dating from about 1803. In 1841 it was bought by Edward Banks, grandson of Sir Edward Banks, a partner in Jolliffe and Banks, building contractors responsible for Southwark, Staines and London Bridges, the latter eventually being sent to the USA. Edward Banks the younger was a local benefactor and in 1877 gave land on which the village school was built, as well as being financially involved in the restoration of the church at that time. He was also a top British specialist on fuchsias and in the 19th century one of the largest cultivators of this plant in the world. During his career he introduced 177 new varieties, including Perfection, 1848, Beauty of Sholden, 1868, and Forget-Me-Not, 1866, the latter being the emblem of the British Fuchsia Society. His career had started shortly after his marriage at East Langdon church in 1841 and his moving into Sholden Lodge as it was then called. Owing to poor health he started cultivating this plant in greenhouses in the Lodge grounds and soon his new varieties were popular, Queen Victoria being photographed with a display of Banks' fuchsias. In Sholden church are several windows and memorial tablets to the Banks family. One of them in the nave is to Mary Henrietta Banks who died in 1846 aged four years and three months, daughter of Edward Banks of Sholden Lodge. Could he have had her in mind when he named these varieties? Banks died in January 1910, aged 90, and was interred in the family vault in the churchyard. Sholden Lodge in the First World War became an auxiliary hospital and Banks' other daughters were nurses there. Today it is a residential home for elderly people.

Shorne

To the east of Green Farm in the north of the parish is the site of another of Kent's 'lost' villages (see *Hope All Saints, Orgarswick, Eastbridge*). Known as Merston, not to be confused with Murston near Sittingbourne, it was a stockaded village in the Saxon period, but an archaeological 'dig' in 1957 also exposed a small Norman church's foundations. By 1445, however, the village was uninhabited, why so is a mystery.

In comparison with this disappearance are the efforts of Tufnell Carbonell Barratt, builder(!) in the 19th century. On the east side of Shorne he recovered an impassable bog and made it into land suitable for building and cultivation. On one part he built himself a house, Port Lodge, after this erecting 'many neat "Swiss" and "Elizabethan" cottages, that has given to that part of the village near his residence an air of rural, picturesque beauty'. A description like a modern estate agent's blurb.

Another instance with a modern ring to it: at Shorne in 1847, as competition to the local inns, a John Beckingham ran . . . The Beef Steak House.

Sissinghurst

In the summer of 1912 the residents of Sissinghurst founded a club for the destruction of flies that were pests. The bodies were produced at club meetings before being destroyed and, according to the *Kentish Gazette*, 24th August 1912, up to that date over 20,000 flies had been killed. The best method of catching them apparently was to coat woodwork and glass with some paraffin, the smell attracting the flies, which were then overcome by the fumes and could easily be captured (see *Borden, Eastry*).

Sittingbourne

It is worth the trouble finding the Dolphin Yard at the end of a bumpy, pot-holed road leading from Sittingbourne's Crown Quay Lane, especially for the maritime enthusiast. Dolphin Yard was formerly the barge yard at cement and brick makers Charles Burley, alongside it being Burley's Dolphin Brand Cement Works. It is located on a tidal inlet running from Sittingbourne and Milton to the Swale, the channel separating the Isle of Sheppey from the Kent mainland whose inlet is fed by the Bourne, one of three streams that flow into it.

The heyday of the area was the early 19th century, when in the wake of the Industrial Revolution it was a port from which Kent produce was transported to the London markets, and there were paper mills, cement works and brickfields. Barges brought in sand, mud, 'rough stuff' (waste, cinders, etc, from households) for brick making and took away the bricks produced. Over 500 sailing barges are believed to have been built in this area, but after the Second World War it declined. Only Burley continued by repairing barges until about 1965, then by 1968 the site was owned by a concrete products manufacturer, Bourncrete.

A barge enthusiast member of the Thames Spritsail Barge Research Group, Tony Ellis, was in the area listing the barge hulks along the creeks and inlets before they were forgotten. The barge yard was rapidly becoming derelict, the inlet basin for barges silting up, but seeing its potential he obtained permission from Bourncrete to use the site for the museum. The first priority was to make watertight and restore the 200 year old wooden shed used as sail loft and forge, then to reopen the silted basin to allow barges in again. So the Dolphin Yard Sailing Barge Museum was born to conserve what is left of the barge building trade.

Today the visitor can see the original barge yard, with forge and its original bellows and furnace, shipwright's shop, sail loft and the original tools used, plus exhibits of the history of the other local industries. There are also sailing barges, including the *Cambria*, the very famous barge skippered by Bob Roberts. This, the last Thames barge to operate without a motor, is on loan from the National Maritime Trust. It is open to the public, who can see the skipper's cabin and hold and get the feel of what life was like aboard. There is a free car park. The Dolphin Yard is open Sundays and bank holidays, 11 to 5, Easter to the end of October, though it will open after then for guided student groups and parties – contact Peter Morgan, Sittingbourne 423215 (see *Kingsnorth*).

To the west of the Dolphin Yard is another preserved part of Sittingbourne's industrial history worth finding, the Sittingbourne and Kemsley Light Railway, Its origins are in the building of a paper mill in 1877 by Edward Lloyd, between Sittingbourne and Milton Creek, the raw material for the paper mill coming by barges that took away the finished paper. A wharf was built and a narrow-gauge, horse-drawn tramway laid to carry to and from the creek. In 1906 the first steam locomotive *Premier* came into service, followed the same year by *Leader* and in 1908 *Excelsior*.

Expansion in the paper industry here meant a new dock at Ridham, four miles from Sittingbourne, the narrow-gauge railway being extended to serve the dock. In the 1920s a new mill meant further expansion and by 1960 there were 13 steam locomotives, one diesel locomotive and 400 wagons, the line extending for about 14 track miles. In 1948 Lloyds was absorbed by the Bowater Group but the railway continued and as Ridham Dock was remote and few workers had cars, coaches built at the Kemsley Mill workshops were added to carry passengers. As national steam railway routes closed enthusiasts became interested in Bowater's railway and parties were allowed to ride on it.

In 1965 a time and motion study said the railway was 'totally uneconomic' and advised the use of lorries, so the railway closed in 1969, when Bowaters Group handed it over to the Locomotive Club of Great Britain to preserve. Various developments took place to open it to the public, but in the mid-1970s a group of railway enthusiasts took over from LCGB and to run it established the Sittingbourne and Kemsley Light Railway Ltd. It is now open Easter to mid-October, every Sunday and bank holiday, in that period, also Christmas, Tuesday and Saturday in July and August. Several steam locomotives are in use or on display including the original *Premier* and *Leader*, plus two diesel engines, ex-Bowater coaches and wagons and four coaches from the Chattenden and Upnor Railway – a Hoo Peninsula line operated first for the Admiralty, then the Royal Engineers, before being closed in 1961.

Smarden

Numerous theories have been offered for the grotesque head on the north wall of the church's nave near to its easternmost window, at a height of approximately eight ft from the floor, supported by two corbels. It is truncated and egg shaped with emphasized eyebrows. The mouth is wide and also exaggerated, two hands either side of it stretching it into a grimace. Surprisingly for the interior of a Christian church it is probably a pagan object, probably a form of the sheil-na-gig or sheila-na-gig, a type of mother goddess. The prominent breasts and exaggerated pudenda – external organs of generation, is an indication of this. These occur numerously in varied forms in churches and religious buildings in western France. In the 12th century England and Normandy were closely linked, so it is feasible English masons took some motif ideas from their Normandy counterparts.

However, it has alternatively been suggested that it symbolises a fearful sexual war goddess. The purpose of either is by its frightening and bizarre expression to repel the 'evil eye' of the Devil and his associates from the interior of the church and to protect worshippers. Its siting at Smarden is curious and uncommon because these grotesque heads and similar figures, beasts, etc are usually carved on the exterior of the church, on or near the entrance, to deal with the 'evil eye' in the churchyard (see *Grain*).

There is also another possible connection of this place with France; the timber-framed properties immediately behind the church, instead of common black and white, have brown timbers and ochre infilling, as in Normandy.

A modern penthouse is a projecting shelter or canopy. At Smarden from the main street the churchyard is entered by passing under the first storey of an overhanging building. Its name – The Pent House.

Snargate

▅ In St Dunstan's church is an example from the days when men were proud to append their name to their work (see *Sturry*). There are two lead sheets taken from the church roof during repairs. One bears the embossed inscription, 'J. Bourne, C. Warden – Warrington Romney plumber T. Apps carpenter and all his jolly men 1780'.

Anne Roper in her *The Gift of the Sea – Romney Marsh* (Birlings, 1984) informs that 'On the Appledore Road is an 18th century house built of brick. In the west wall facing the road a single brick is stamped with the word DRAIN. A tax in 1784 was levied on bricks, the only bricks exempt from it being those for drainage purposes, used by builders and farmers, these bricks having to be stamped with DRAIN. The tax was abolished in 1850.' This Drain brick was the only one Anne Roper discovered during her lifetime on the Marsh. It would be interesting to know of others surviving.

Snave

▅ St. Augustine's church is known as 'the Daffodil church' (See *Lower Hardres*). The name arose after a visitor felt the lonely church 'needed some happiness to enfold it', so sent 500 daffodil bulbs for the churchyard which have multiplied. Snave is one of the 23 Manors of the Romney Marsh so had the right to erect its own gallows as one of its privileges. Near Walnut Tree Farm, Snave, is Hangman's Toll Bridge that may or may not have been associated with these gallows. The bridge is associated with men who were hanged, their bodies being brought to Hangman's Field, Snave Wick, for interment; the toll to cross the bridge to enter the field with the corpses being paid by the hangman. The number thus interred is unknown: two headstones survive, which were recovered from one of the dykes around the field.

Southborough

In 1829 Sir David Salomons purchased a small elegant villa called Broomhill in extensive grounds south-west of Southborough. A wealthy financier, he enlarged and rebuilt it making it into a large country house. Among his many offices was Sheriff of Kent in 1839, and first Jewish Lord Mayor of London in 1855. On his death in 1873 Broomhill passed to his nephew, David Lionel Salomons (1851-1925). His interests were wide: 'scientific research, four in hand coach driving, designing motor carriages, mechanical work generally'. He invented the world's first electric automobile, made from a tricycle and powered with a Bunsen battery. He wrote and lectured on electricity, optics and photography. In 1870 (see *Bishopsbourne*) he invented an electric exposing camera and in 1895 was experimenting with and showing cinematograph films. He invented an automatic railway signalling system and was granted a patent for it in 1874.

At the north-east of the house, acting as his own architect, he completed the yellow and red-brick water tower, with a round turret, both battlemented. On top was a mounting for a telescope. Between 1890-94 the fantastic red-brick stables he designed were built to resemble a French hotel rather than to house 21 horses. They were ahead of their time with an automatic watering and feeding system for the horses, with hot water heating and lit by electricity. There was a coach house for twelve drags, the largest size carriages, but from 1895, when his interest turned to motor carriages, the stables were used less often, but until the 1950s one of the drags remained in the coach house, before being moved to Maidstone's Tyrwhitt-Drake Museum of Carriages, where it is still on display.

In 1894-96 the Science Theatre was built, 80 ft long, 40 ft wide, the largest privately constructed theatre in England at that time. Attached to it was a photographic studio, darkrooms and chemical laboratory. In the Science Theatre, so-called because Salomons also demonstrated his scientific inventions to friends there, is a Welte Philharmonic organ, the only one of its type now surviving as the other example at the Welte & Sohn factory in Germany was destroyed by Second World War bombing. It had cost Salomons £4,050 when installed in 1914. In 1988 a meeting of organ enthusiasts was held in the theatre and a recording of a Welte organ played, after which the curtains were drawn back to reveal Salomons' Welte organ to gasps from the surprised audience.

Even more pioneering was the dynamo Salomons installed in 1896 to supply the house with electricity for 1,000 16-candlepower lights. Broomhill had been the first building to use electricity for cooking and other domestic work.

Sir David Lionel Salomons' only son, David Reginald, was killed in the First World War so the baronetcy became extinct. In 1938 Sir David's last surviving daughter, Vera Salomons, presented the house to Kent County Council, with covenants limiting its use 'as a technical institute, college, museum, memorial hall, public park or as a convalescent home or hospital . . .' It was used as a convalescent home for women from 1938 to 1971, the property passing to the Ministry of Health in 1948 at the start of the National Health Service.

Known since 1938 as David Salomons House the memento rooms are preserved exactly as they were at the turn of the century. They are open free to the public Monday, Wednesday and Friday, 2 to 5 pm. The stables are not open and can only be viewed from outside, and the water tower can only be seen from afar.

Surprisingly this example of a private Victorian theatre had been unchanged and unused as a performance site for many years, still retaining its original fittings, wood panelled interior, deep stage and excellent acoustics. Since the summer of 1992, it has been brought back into use by the Broomhill Trust, with concerts, recitals and opera performances with international performers, as well as being used for other purposes.

Southfleet

In the early 19th century watercress beds were developed at Spring-head, Southfleet, fed by a fleet (stream) arising there. The luxuriant watercress was renowned and sent in great quantities to satisfy a demand from that same London populace, no doubt in need of the plant's iron content, that visited Northfleet's riverside Rosherville Gardens or Gravesend's Windmill Hill for its fresh air. Like Rosherville the name Springhead survives, but the watercress beds do not, closed in the 1930s.

In his will of 1637 the Sheriff of Kent to James I, Sir John Sedley, bequested £500 for the establishing of a free school in Southfleet. The red-brick front of it does still survive and remains in educational use, incorporated in a primary school.

Speldhurst

On Speldhurst Hill the half-timbered George and Dragon inn reputes to be c1212, but it does have some 14th century beams. There are hollows in the stonework at the side of the large fireplace where long ago armed men would call at the inn to quaff an ale and sharpen their swords, daggers and knives while doing so. Legend has it that soldiers returning from the battle of Agincourt in 1415 passed through the village and supped or stayed at the inn. Is there any fact to support this?

Tradition again says that in this battle Sir Richard Waller of Groombridge Place in this parish, captured Charles, Duke of Orleans and brought him back to Groombridge as a royal prisoner. Charles was also supposedly resident there for 20 years until ransomed. One version is that during this time, with the money Sir Richard received for maintaining the French Duke and the ransom, Waller restored St Mary the Virgin church and put the Duke's coat of arms, which had been granted by the Duke to Waller, as a quarter with his own coat of arms on a stone over the church's south porch. A second version is that Charles himself paid for the restoration as a thanksgiving for the friendly maintenance he had received from Waller and the local people. The Orleans Stone is still there, rescued from the 1791 fire that destroyed the church and restored to its proper position, in the third church to be built on the site, 1870-71. As for the Duke, however, the tradition has been disputed, claiming that the hostage was instead the Duke's younger brother Jean, Duke ot Angontime. Despite this it does appear that there were relevant armed men of this time and later in the area to sharpen their swords at the George and Dragon inn.

A Sussex spire was added to the tower in 1923 and on this was fitted the weather vane, that had been on the original church struck by lightning in 1791, and saved from the resulting fire.

The White Ensign flag over the pulpit in the church flew at the masthead of HMS *Warspite* in the Battle of Jutland in May 1916, and was placed in the church on the first anniversary of the battle.

On the outskirts of Speldhurst is Shadwell Wood, in which there are supposed to be five wells, but only one has been found.

Stalisfield Green

➤ Among the coppices of the North Downs in East Kent and in the High Weald charcoal production took place. It did so here in the Arketts Farm area at the turn of the century and possibly up to the 1920s, carried on in the traditional practice. This involved the building of the three ft or so lengths of cordwood into several cone-shaped seven ft high stacks 20 yards in circumference at their base, covered with dampened rough grass and bracken on which damp earth, old ashes, sand, sometimes wetted turf, were placed to exclude air from outside. The wood used was from cants of underwood in plantations, the charcoal burner having in early winter bought wood sometimes too crooked to use for hop poles and gate posts.

In spring, after the woodmen had felled any oak trees in a woodland and flayed bark from the trunks and large branches, this bark was transported to tanneries at Canterbury and Ashford for tanning leather. The leftover branches were sawn into lengths and used by the charcoal burner, while the trunk went to timber yards to season. He also bought fruit trees if an orchard was being 'grubbed up' (cleared), cutting trunks and branches into cordwood lengths. The charring length of time depended on the wood species – oak, hornbeam and other hard woods, six to seven days; sweet chestnut, beech, apple, etc would be charred in three to four days; sere wood – old hop poles, fencing, etc – charred in a day to a day and a half.

The smokeless, odourless charcoal produced was used mainly in hop oasthouses, the hop driers preferring charcoal for their kilns. It also went to the gunpowder works at Faversham. Wood only partly charred, known as a 'brand', was bought by housewives for their cooking stoves and washhouse boiler fires. In the First World War charcoal from here was also sent to France for use as a fuel in the battle areas. Being smokeless it did not give away the soldiers' position as they tried to keep warm, especially in the bitter winter of 1916-17.

Staple

There are numerous inns named White Horse, Black Horse, Black Bull, Red Cow, Red Lion, etc, but the only example in Kent called The Black Pig is the inn of 1588 in Barnsole Road, Staple. It is puzzling to know why it is the sole one as Kent originally had its own breed, the Kent Black Pig, also called the Black Kent. It has been compared with the Old English Large Black that was descended from the 'Old English Hog' of the 16th century, in turn descended and bred from the wild boars of the Weald (see *Mereworth*), but the Kent Black Pig had smaller, drooping ears, far less hair and it was much finer textured and stood higher off the ground.

Ralph Whitlock gave me his opinion that the Kent Black was possibly a similar breed to the Dorset Black, one of a number of several black breeds confined to southern and eastern counties in the 19th century. A number of these breeds were formed in that period by pig breeders to meet their own and customers' requirements. Most were short-lived, but some survived for a time and were locally popular.

According to the Board of Agriculture and Fisheries *Report on Kent* in 1911, concerning its pigs: 'In no part of the area does the breeding of pigs form a very important feature of the agriculture; there is little or no bacon curing and what pigs are raised are sold in the main for local consumption. None of the old unmixed Kent herds have, however, been registered [with the National Pig Breeders Association to establish herd books for the pedigree herds] so it is probable that they will die out as a separate breed and become merged in the general Large Black breed'. It appears this is what in fact did happen (see *Ivychurch*).

There was also a Kent White Pig, rather long-legged, narrow-backed and similar to the early Suffolk White Pig, with medium length ears, thickly hairy and said to have a thick rind or skin. This presumably went the same way, becoming merged with the Large White breed.

According to a Kent saying a 'Kent Hog' was a Kentish-born man who would give anything away – as long as it was of no further use to him! There are also many Kent dialect words and other expressions associated with the hog or pig.

Apart from its curly tail and straight back the inn sign pig has a fair likeness to a Kent Black Pig which had an almost straight tail and a back tending to slope from its hind quarters down to its shoulders and head.

Staplehurst

This village has evidence of how hard life was in the 'good old days'. At the entrance to All Saints church path a notice states: 'TAKE NOTICE that if any obstruction or inconvenience be occasioned to Foot Passengers by the loitering of Persons on the Pavement leading to the Church, or any annoyance whatever be offered to those who are going to or from Church, the Parish Officers are instructed to summon the Offenders before a Magistrate that they may be punished as the Law directs.' This could indicate that there was a problem, as now, with certain people trouble making, or it was a prior warning not to or else – perhaps some time in the stocks? Either way it was advisable not to hang about near the church on Sundays and other religious days.

In the reign of Roman Catholic Mary I three Protestant Staplehurst women refused to attend the church services. The church priest, Thomas Hendon, reported them to the magistrate, Sir John Baker of Sissinghurst, 'Bloody Baker' who revelled in his official task of persecuting the Protestants. They were found guilty at their 'trial' so Joan Bradbridge, Alice Benden and Alice Potkins were burned at the stake for their beliefs. At the side of the village main street a memorial stone commemorates the religious martyrs.

Incidental to this event there is a tradition that Sir John Baker was returning from Canterbury with a warrant for the execution of two more martyrs when near Cranbrook he learned of Mary's death and the thwarting of his plans. The place is still known as Baker's Cross. Wisely he died a few days after Mary, meanwhile Revd Hendon prudently fled the area.

South of Staplehurst is Lovehurst Manor Farm. At some time in its history it was converted into a moated property by an owner diverting a nearby branch of the wandering river Beult around the property and then making it cross back over itself and carry on its original course.

The road east from Staplehurst to Frittenden, off the Roman road

A229, was always known to local people as 'Frittenden Brass Band', but now no one knows why.

Stockbury

➤ Opposite the north side of St Mary Magdalene churchyard, across the road that leads westwards to the village, is a grass pasture known as Bell Meadow. I wonder if anyone has ever investigated below its surface? If close to a church, areas with this name, Bell Field, or similar, often signify that it is the site where a bell or bells were cast for the church. In the days when rural highways were in poor condition for part of the year, instead of casting a bell in the nearest town or city and hauling it to the customer church, the bell-founders would take their equipment and materials needed, find a suitable area nearest to the church, with a supply of timber in the vicinity, then cast the bell on this site. An example is that at Newchurch. During the digging of a grave there in 1973 a 'bell pit', believed to have been used for the casting of the church's original bells, was discovered.

Although hardly hidden, Stockbury church's weather vane may be overlooked. On this is the date 1676, possibly the year the first vane was erected. During the 1987 hurricane the weather vane then in situ, not thought to be 17th century either despite the date on it, was blown down and damaged. A local historian, W.T. Buck, generously provided the funds for a local craftsman-ironworker, Jack Cockett at Yelsted, a hamlet in the parish, to provide the replica replacement.

In the churchyard, near an old yew showing signs of having experienced many gales on this exposed hilltop overlooking the Stockbury Valley, is a headstone that is possibly the oldest in a Kent churchyard still legible. On the 2½ ft high headstone the inscription, surmounted by a skull and crossbones, is all in capital letters. It reads 'Here Lieth the Body of Thomas, the Sonn of Thomas and Elizabeth Gover, who departed this life the Fifteenth of November, 1620, being aged 26 years and 3 months. This young man the people loved. He changed this Life for Heaven above.' Almost certainly the yew tree's cover has protected the lettering from erosion.

In the church if you stand high up close to and directly in front of the organ on its raised platform under the tower arch, by looking downwards and eastwards up the nave to the chancel it is possible to see how the tower and nave are not in alignment, but whether accidental or deliberate is unknown (see *Keston, Cuxton*).

Sturry

➤The village name has its origin in Esturai, derived from Aestur, an ancient name for the Stour. It could be called 'the village with three bridges', all of them within a few yards of each other. Two convey the A28 Canterbury-Thanet road over the Stour where it divides into two parts. In the 18th century one part was crossed by a medieval bridge, the other part was a ford. In 1768 'because the fording of the river at Sturry is attended with many inconveniences and frequently impracticable, whereby the communication with the Isle of Thanet is greatly obstructed' it was proposed to raise a public subscription to build a bridge there. 'A lofty brick bridge' was built in 1776 near to the Black Mill and 'overcame the dangers of the ford'.

As may be guessed this improvement increased traffic through Sturry. The traffic had a parlous effect on the medieval bridge, and soon it became essential to replace it. In 1834 it was demolished and replaced by the five-arched red-brick bridge used today. J. Moys, builder, and I. Hacker, mason, no doubt were proud to have their names incised on the capstones of the fifth and sixth parapet piers after completing its construction. Their names are still clear-cut, visible from the footbridge adjoining the road bridge, while on bricks at the east end of the same north side the name W. Crux and mason's initials I.H. with year 1834 are also to be seen. This bridge became known as White Mill Bridge as it was close to the mill of that name. In 1971 the road was realigned south of the 1776 Black Mill Bridge, and close to the site of the demolished Black Mill a third bridge was built to supersede the 1776 bridge. Though the two bridges are still parallel this new bridge eliminates a hazardous dog-leg bend caused by the original route to the 18th century bridge.

If a visitor from the Canterbury direction turns from the A28 first left past the Belisha crossing, then proceeds a few yards through the modern part of the High Street built on the bombed ruins of this part of the village, they will find the surviving part of the old High Street hidden around the corner, where tranquillity reigns. The upper front wall of Franklyn House, in the new High Street, has a black and white lettered plaque stating 'This plaque is to commemorate the Bombing of Sturry and those who died in November 1941'. A wall tablet in the church lists their names.

In the old High Street, outside the Swan inn, stands a short four-sided milestone. One incised face states 'Ramsgate 14 m', another 'London 58 m', the other two faces, if they ever bore anything, now being blank. Notable is that the milestone bears a ring on its summit,

Milestone with ring, Sturry High Street

perhaps for tethering ponies and horses of callers at the inn? On one occasion I saw it used differently, to tether an excited dog whose owner was obviously purchasing in the butcher's shop next door to the inn!

In 1992 there was excitement hereabouts when a seal made its way from the sea up the Stour, reaching the millpool in front of the now tree-covered site of the demolished White Mill. To the considerable consternation of anglers and entertainment of local people, watching from the footbridge adjoining Mr Moys' White Mill Bridge, the seal disported itself in the trout-rich water until this became too much for the anglers and river authority. The seal showed no sign of leaving of its own accord so it was captured and taken back to whence it came, not too soon for the anglers and surviving fish.

Sutton Valence

Sutton Valence was another of the places in Kent where a curious wager took place (see *Biddenden*) A Johnny Lee, from a Romany family, claimed he could walk for eight hours without stopping up and down a street in the village during St Edmund's Day Fair, held annually on 20th November. This might be thought a perfectly manageable task, but Lee would also be carrying a heavy brick in each hand! Wagers were placed on him and so on the Fair day, 1782, he set off. For six hours he walked non-stop, fed by lumps of cheese placed in his mouth by his wife. During a short absence by her, however, someone offered Johnny a glass of rum 'to sustain his strength', which he drank on the trot. Alas, being tired and 'void in the stomach' this had the opposite effect, that of making him 'swimmy-headed', then he reeled and fell down in the street, unable to rise until he had slept awhile. The aftermath is not recorded but it is assumed all wagers backing him to succeed were lost.

John Willes (1777-1852), who re-introduced round-arm bowling into cricket, lived for a time at Bellingham House. Born at Headcorn he farmed early in life in the Tonford area of Canterbury. He practised cricket in a barn with his sister Christina, not his wife as is usually stated, bowling to him. It is reputed that Christina, depending on what she was wearing, used to bowl to him underarm as was the rule, but when wearing a crinoline type dress she found her bowling arm obstructed by her wide flowing skirt. Frustrated she whirled the ball over her head and to her and John's surprise she sent down a ball almost twice as fast. Impressed, he decided to re-introduce round-arm bowling. Another bowler had in fact attempted it for a short time several years earlier but failed probably due to hostile opposition.

In a match at Lords between Kent and the MCC in 1822, Willes bowled round-arm and was 'no-balled'. He tried again and was 'no-balled' again, so threw the ball down, jumped on his horse and rode home saying he would never play cricket again. When opposition to this bowling style was overcome he did play again and even taught the great Alfred Mynn (1807-61), who was known as 'The Lion of Kent', playing a total of 99 matches in the Kent XI from 1834 to 1859. Mynn was interred at Thurnham. Willes was also considered the best shot and amateur boxer in Kent of his time, additionally keeping hounds and fox hunting. He died at Gloucester but is interred to the left side of the church path in St Mary's churchyard.

The Motto Cottages near The Clothworkers Arms are so-called because each bears a tablet on its wall with a religious quotation, but not a motto. It is said the builder had strong religious principles and wanted to thus spread the Word of God.

Tankerton-on-Sea

➤ According to the saying 'an Englishman's home is his castle'. This was true in one sense concerning those men who lived at Tankerton 'Castle', built at the eastern end of Harbour Street, Whitstable, where the rising ground, known as Tankerton Slopes, starts. The oldest surviving part, the central tower, dates back only to the 1790s, built by a London businessman, Charles Pearson. He used it as a summer residence by the sea as did later owners. In 1820 it was added to by his son, also Charles, but business difficulties forced its sale to a wealthy London silk merchant, Wynn Ellis, a millionaire, a Kent magistrate and eventually an MP. It was described at this time as 'Tankerton Tower set on a cliff of the sea, commands a prospect of the ocean, beautified with tasteful pleasure grounds.' Ellis added to the belltower and long west front, also having the grounds landscaped. For a time he installed his mistress, Susan Lloyd, in the 'Castle'. He died in 1875.

Adjoining the 'Castle' grounds Ellis had constructed almshouses in 1873 in memory of his wife Mary, and paid their upkeep, this and other good deeds perhaps salving his later conscience for his earlier moral misdemeanours. The house, estate and title, Lord of the Manor, according to one source, were left to his children. Eventually one of them, Sydney, sold to the Tankerton Estate Company in 1890. Another source states the 'Castle' and estate were bequeathed to his mistress 'to Miss S.A. Lloyd for life', which could be construed as payment 'for services rendered'. A Thomas Adams bought it in 1897, called it 'The Towers' and built the impressive gatehouse. In 1935 Whitstable Urban District Council bought it for local government offices, the grounds that year being opened to the public to commemorate the Royal Silver Jubilee. In 1972 when Canterbury City Council took over the area's local government the 'Castle' was developed as a community centre, as it still is.

For centuries the Tankerton Slopes, descending to a shingle beach, with the wide prospect of the sea, were and still are enjoyed by the public. Here have been and continue to be held occasional festivities on the level top while some of the Slopes are left wild. In one such section, the rough terrain between Marine Parade and the sea, a very rare plant occurs and with it an equally rare moth, both now protected by law, the area being designated a Site of Special Scientific Interest in 1986.

According to John Gerard (1545-1612), author of the famous *Herball*, the first record in Kent of hog's fennel was in 1597 'at Whitstable in Kent in a medow neere to the sea side . . . It groweth also in great plentie at Feversham in Kent, neere unto the haven upon the bankes thereof and the meadowes adjoining.'

The hog's fennel (*Peucedanum officinale*), also called Sulphur Weed, originally extended from what is now near the site of the Tankerton Hotel eastwards to what is called Priest and Sow Corner, Tankerton, but necessary drainage to the Slopes has entailed restriction of its growing area. It is a member of the *Umbelliferae*, the carrot family, related to the hedge parsley, wild celery, hemlock, angelica and

165

others. The erect stems grow to three ft high, with large umbels of pale yellow flowers, the leaves being ternate (three times divided). It also still occurs in Faversham Creek, both sites being known to be almost 400 years in existence.

The associated rare moth, *Agonopterix putridella*, lays its eggs on the hog's fennel, the resulting brown-headed dark green caterpillar, 12 mm long when fully grown, only feeding on this plant. It makes a cocoon of leaves in which to pupate. The buff coloured moth has a wing span of 12 to 15 mm, flying only at dusk and by day staying among the foliage. In recent years a related plant, alexanders, also with umbels of yellow flowers, but broader leaves, has invaded the site. Every summer Kent Trust for Nature Conservation volunteers cut back the alexanders to prevent it taking over the site.

Tenterden

➤ Originally called The Old Meeting House, built about 1695 on the site of a barn in what is now Ashford Road, the brick Unitarian chapel has a plaque on the front wall noting that an American statesman, philosopher and scientist, Dr Benjamin Franklin, worshipped here in 1783. Franklin was apprenticed in the printing trade as a typesetter, worked on his brother's newspaper, then came to England to work in a London printing office for 18 months, returning to America to establish his own newspaper. He was interested in science and experimented with electricity and other phenomena, inventing the lightning conductor. When appointed agent for several American provinces he lived in England for 18 years and during this time the Royal Society elected him a Fellow.

It was also while living here that he met his friend, Dr Joseph Priestley, a leading Unitarian who preached in the Meeting House while Franklin was among the congregation. Priestley is famous as the discoverer of oxygen and other gases, also for writing *A History of Electricity*. Like Franklin he was also a vociferous advocate of freedom and progress. The interior of the chapel still retains the original woodwork from when it was rebuilt in 1746, with galleries on three sides, the pulpit and chairs railed off on the fourth side.

One of the vicars of St Mildred's parish church was the Revd Philip Ward, from 1830 until his death in 1859. What makes him notable is that he married the illegitimate daughter of Lord Nelson and Lady Hamilton, Horatia. Four of Horatia and Philip Ward's eight children were born in the old vicarage that stood just behind the present vicarage. One of his sons, Horatio Nelson Ward was his father's curate from 1848 to 1853. On his death Revd Ward was interred in the family churchyard vault between the chancel and the Woolpack Inn. Horatia then moved to Pinner where she died in 1881 aged 80. A stained glass window was installed in the Lady Chapel by parishioners in the Revd Ward's memory but the Bishop of Dover in 1930 thought a representation of the Devil in the window was inappropriate for a Lady Chapel and so it was replaced by the window there now.

St Mildred's church was one of the churches in the 1588 system of beacons warning of the Spanish Armada approach, taking its signal from Fairlight near Hastings. It was on the church's high tower and was 'a sort of iron kettle, holding about a gallon, with a ring or loop of the same metal around the upper part of it to hold coal, resin, etc, being hung at the end of a piece of timber about 8 ft long.' The four pinnacles on the tower each have a vane, first placed there in 1682. The tower's square-headed west doorway with double doors is one of only two in Kent, the other being at Lydd.

Possibly the oldest building in Tenterden is 91 High Street, Pittlesden Gatehouse, a tiny half-timbered, hipped roof property with widely spaced timbers and though often said to be 15th century its construction suggests it might be the 14th century, and may have been the gatehouse to a long lost 14th century mansion.

Teynham

No record has so far been found giving a date *when* cherries were first introduced into Kent for cultivation; *where* they were first planted is more certain, Teynham. William Lambarde in his *Perambulation of Kent*, 1570, wrote 'This Tenham, with thirty other parishes extending from Rainham to Blean Wood, be the Cherry Garden and Apple Orchard of Kent, but as this at Tenham is the parent of all the rest and from whom they have drawn the good juice of all their pleasant fruit, so it is also the most large, delightsome and beautiful of them . . . Here our honest patriot, Richard Harries, fruiterer to Henry VIII, planted by his great cost and rare industry the sweet cherry, the temperate pippin and golden renate. He about the year 1533 obtained 105 acres of good ground in the parish of Tenham, then called The Brennet, which he divided into ten parcels and with great care, good choice and no small labour and cost, brought plants from beyond the seas and furnished this ground with them, so beautifully, as they not only stand in most right line, but seem to be of one sort, shape and fashion, as if they had been drawn through one mould . . .' Lambarde then gives a clue that Harris was not the first to do this, indicating Harris had brought in new stock as 'the plants our ancestors had brought out of Normandy had lost their native verdour'. William Camden, another antiquarian author, writing in 1586 stated 'Then I saw Tenham, the parent as it were of all the choice fruit gardens and orchards of Kent and the most large and delightfulsome of them all, planted in the time of Henry the Eighth by Richard Harris, his fruiterer . . .' Edward Hasted, in his *The History and Topographical Survey of the County of Kent*, Vol XII, 1801, wrote with the same thoughts: 'In his reign [Henry VIII] were cherry orchards first planted here, with a more improved kind of fruit, brought from Flanders by one Harris, another of this king's gardeners . . .'

So there is no doubt Teynham is where cherry *orchards* were first planted and by Harris. Two sites have been suggested. One is the area known as New Gardens, now mostly a housing estate, that local tradition says was originally Teynham Manor church land seized by Henry VIII, who gave it to Harris for cultivating cherries. The second site is Osier Farm, near the present stream, where osiers grew, hence its name.

The Manor Rolls refer to New Gardens as The Brennet, the name used by Lambarde. Elizabeth Selby in her book *Teynham Manor and Hundred*, felt the case for Osier Farm being the first site was strengthened by there being a pencil note in the Manor Rolls stating 'Oziers Farm was The Brennet'. It is fact that what is now New Gardens was originally called The Teynham Outlands, an outlying area of the Archbishop's Manor. If it *was* the second area Harris cultivated with cherry orchard, after planting The Brennet (Osiers Farm) first, which has been suggested, then New Gardens would have been an appropriate name for it.

There is no denying Harris planted the first cherry *orchards* at Teynham, perhaps also the first on a commercial basis, but he was not the first to plant cherry trees in numbers in Kent, a fact so many Kent writers overlook through relying on Lambarde's comments.

According to the *Reeve's Accounts of the Manor of Teynham* dated about 1376 (a reeve being a bailiff or steward of a manor) 20 pence as payment for 'ciresis' (an early spelling of cherries) is listed, 'besides cherries sent to our Lord'. Teynham Manor, with its archiepiscopal palace, was 'church land' belonging to the Archbishop and Christ Church, Canterbury, or 'demesne land', landed property kept in the owner's hands for his own use, ie, the archbishop, not let to tenants. From the *Accounts*, however, it is unclear if the manor received 20 pence as income from someone buying cherries from it, or if the 20 pence is expenditure the reeve paid out to someone growing cherries locally to be given to the archbishop. Did Christ Church, Canterbury, cultivate cherries on their land at the manor or employ others to do so and sell part of the cherry produce, or were there cherry trees in private cultivation outside the boundary of the Teynham Manor from where the reeve purchased the cherries? Whichever of these is true the reference in the *Reeve's Accounts* indicates cherries were being cultivated in quantity at Teynham in the 14th century – long before Harris arrived on the scene.

The *Reeve's Accounts* reference to 'cherries sent to our Lord' is easier to explain. These were certainly cherries that were sent to the archbishop as a gift. The gift would have had no religious purpose and it was normal practice in the late Middle Ages. No doubt cherries from a local orchard would have been appreciated as a change from the often monotonous food that must have been the lot of even archbishops at that time.

The site of the archbishop's manor is known, north of Teynham railway station, between Teynham Court and Conyer.

Thanington

At Tonford Lane, Thanington, the passer-by can see and use a Dutch bridge made of an African wood spanning an English river. It replaced a single-level Victorian wagon-type footbridge, in which the wooden sides are slightly angled away from the central footway across it and resemble a wood-sided horse-drawn farm wagon. In 1987 this latter footbridge was swept off its foundations by strong winds and floodwater against it, to carry it into the Stour where it was damaged beyond repair. In 1988 the present footbridge was built by Kent County Council's Direct Labour Organisation. It was obtained through Sarum Hardwood Structures, Winchester, from their parent company Dutch bridge designers and makers, Groot Lemmer, of Lemmer, Netherlands. The main span is 22.1 m and the footway width 1.5 m, reached up six wide steps on both sides of the river bank. The hardwood timber used is Ekki Lophira Azobe, commonly known as Red Ironwood, from the rain forests and swamps of the Cameroons, West Africa, an extremely hard, heavy and durable, decay and disease resistant wood, with an expected life span of use in this bridge of at least 50 years. Some of the boys who now fish from it could see their sons do the same.

Tonbridge

In 1752 Horace Walpole, the author whose letters give a graphic picture of Georgian England, went on a tour of Kent. In a letter to a friend, Richard Bentley, he wrote 'We lay that night at Tunbridge town and were surprised with the ruins of the old castle. The gateway is perfect and the inclosure formed into a vineyard by a Mr Hooker to whom it belongs and the walls spread with fruit and the mount on which the keep stood planted in the same way. The prospect is charming and a breach in the wall opens below to a pretty Gothic Bridge of three arches over the Medway. We honoured the man for his taste . . . But, alas, he sometimes makes eighteen sour hogsheads and is going to disrobe the ivy-mantled tower, because it harbours birds! The inn was full of farmers and tobacco . . .'

It is to be wondered where he stayed. Could it have been the 15th century half-timbered Chequers Inn described by Walter Jerrold in his *Highways and Byways in Kent*, 1907, 'the well preserved three hundred years old Chequers Inn, which is strikingly picturesque from the street and the internal arrangement of which shows the spacious arched rooms – now divided up by partitions – in which our forefathers took their rest within their inn in days presumably before the refinement of separate rooms for guests had been reached'. He also reported 'An old visitor objected to the removal of the ivy from the ruins – a present day visitor may well complain of the coloured lights with which they are hung'.

At the top of the High Street and off it to the right is Bordyke, 'the borough ditch', claimed now to be the most attractive street in the town. Here in Bordyke House lived Miss Eliza Acton (1799-1859), the poetess cum cookery writer of the 19th century. She started as a poetess, presenting some of her verses to Queen Adelaide when the latter visited the town in 1837. However, in 1845 her *Modern Cookery* was published and became the most popular cookery book of its day, owing to its appearance just at the time when the commercial food industry was beginning. Surprisingly her popularity continued even after Mrs Beeton published her first edition of her cookery book in 1861. Eliza Acton tested most of the recipes she published on her own kitchen stove and those she didn't came from friends and relatives who reliably confirmed their sources.

Tonbridge School faces the High Street and it has connections with a more famous literary lady. Jane Austen's father, the Revd George Austen was a master there for some time.

Being near the river generations of Tonbridge pupils have rowed on or bathed in the Medway here. Robert Goodsall in his *The Medway and its Tributaries*, 1955, reminds us that river pollution is not a modern hazard. He refers to a critic who wrote in 1870: 'We cannot doubt that the place called the Locks is very fit for bathing, but when barges go down the river they always bring down the tar with them and it is not pleasant to find oneself covered with tar. Secondly, the water is not nearly so clear as it is above the town'.

Near Tonbridge is a bridge over the Medway known as 'Lucifer Bridge'. It got this name because the then 19th century Lord de L'Isle who owned the land surrounding it erected barriers to prevent local people bathing in, boating or skating on the river. The local populace were not happy with this and removed the barriers. One protester marked the event by writing on the bridge 'How art thou fallen from Heaven, O'Lucifer' (Isaiah 14 v. 12). Lord de L'Isle decided not to continue with blocking the river, but the name stuck for the bridge.

Trottiscliffe

Near the green in the weatherboarded White House, Trottiscliffe (pronouned Tros-lee), the painter, designer, engraver and official war artist Graham Sutherland lived for a number of years. During this period he was influenced by Samuel Palmer, the artist, who had lived at nearby Shoreham, and Sutherland became known for his surrealist landscapes. His portraits, because of the attitudes of the sitters, were sometimes controversial, notably the 80th birthday portrait of Sir Winston Churchill and that of Somerset Maugham. He also designed the large tapestry 'Christ in Majesty' for Coventry Cathedral in 1962. He died in 1980 aged 77 and is interred in St Peter and St Paul's churchyard, Trottiscliffe.

Tudeley

Unless already told, anyone visiting for the first time Tudeley's tiny 18th century All Saints red-brick church, located beyond a farmyard and sitting on its original medieval foundations, can have no realisation of the colourful splendour in glass they are about to witness. Numerous churches have examples of brilliant stained glass windows of various ages or modern forms of religious art, sculpture and so on, but Tudeley's glass has been claimed to be finer than that in Coventry and Canterbury cathedrals for detail and resplendent entirety.

It owes its origin to a sad tragedy. In 1963 Sarah, daughter of Sir Henry and Lady d'Avigdor-Goldsmid of Somerhill, the Jacobean house in the parish, was drowned at sea in a sailing accident. To commemorate her Marc Chagall, the French painter and stained glass window designer, was commissioned to create an east window in the church. Chagall had previously designed windows in the Rheims and Metz cathedrals and the Hospital Synagogue in Jerusalem. A vision of a dominant Christ on the Cross is depicted under a nimbus-like red rainbow, adjoined by mourning women and angels. A young woman is shown adrift in waves that merge with Heaven's blue, the shape of the glass suggesting the movement of the sea. She is also to be seen on a ladder climbing to Heaven and on a red horse at the foot of the Cross, symbolising happiness. There are also animals among vegetation and fleeting angels.

From the first commission for one, the east, window the project expanded to twelve, the last of the windows being put into position in 1985, the year that Chagall died. Even Chichester cathedral has only one Chagall window, Tudeley's number being unique in England. They should be seen on a sunny day. Blue is the main colour which is heightened in effect by the 18th century green marbled barrel-vaulted ceiling of the nave. The five windows in the chancel are blue but one quatrefoil light, an ornamental figure, is yellow. In the south aisle the windows are yellow, blazingly intensified when the sun shines through them. The beauty of Chagall's creation is a priceless and permanently fitting tribute to this lost daughter.

Tunbridge Wells

➤ Today the Showfields Housing Estate built after the Second World War is a pleasant area of residential accommodation. It was previously part of the Marquis of Abergavenny's Eridge Estate off the Eridge Road near the West railway station, until purchased by the Tunbridge Wells Agricultural Society for their Show Ground. However, in 1894 history was made here for it was also the site of the first Motor Show in Kent and England. The Horseless Carriage Exhibition took place on Tuesday, 15th October, from 3 to 5 pm.

It had been organised by Sir David Lionel Salomons, of Broomhill, Southborough, Mayor of Tunbridge Wells, and who held or had held various other offices – Director of the South-Eastern Railway,

MP for Greenwich, Kent County Councillor for Tonbridge, magistrate, Deputy Lieutenant of Kent and Hon. Colonel of Kent (Fortress) Royal Engineers.

As soon as it began to be a practical proposition he was enthusiastic about the motorised vehicle. Expert on motor mechanics he had designed motor carriages and invented the world's first electric automobile (see *Southborough*). At Broomhill in place of some old stables he built what is probably now the finest example of early motor-carriage 'houses' anywhere in Britain. Outside Broomhill's Science Theatre the five garages, to use their modern name, still have their original doors and hinges. He had thought of all angles, from cavity walls to central heating, tongued and grooved boarded ceilings, inspection pits at just the correct depth for the chauffeur to stand in. He also contributed a chapter on 'The Motor Stable and its Management' for the book *Motors and Motor Driving*, by Alfred C. Harmsworth, published in 1902, another contributor being the Hon C.S. Rolls of Rolls-Royce fame.

Salomons decided to organise an exhibition of the vehicles available to the public but the public was sceptical. The problem was finding enough vehicles to exhibit! He went to Paris and bought a 3¾ hp single-cylinder, rear-engined Peugeot car, with tube ignition, solid tyres and tiller steering. Friends and relatives who owned relevant vehicles were persuaded to take part, and European makers were persuaded to advertise their product by showing one at Tunbridge Wells. Some of the makers, Count de Dion of Paris among them, also attended.

Among other vehicles there was a Panhard with Daimler engine; a de Dion Tricycle with petroleum motor; a 'Steam Horse' (a form of traction engine) attached to a landau, by de Dion & Bouton; a Vis-a-Vis by Peugeot; even a fire engine with a Daimler engine made by Panhard and Levassor. The vehicles entered the enclosure at three o'clock. Admission for the public was one shilling (5p).

A few hundred curious public were hoped for. On the day thousands arrived from London and surrounding counties to see the strange sight of a collection of vehicles moving under power without horses hauling them. Demonstrations took place, although the soft ground was announced as unsuitable for the solid tyred vehicles used to hard roads.

Salomons in his Vis-a-Vis drove round and round the show ground, stopping occasionally to show the public the 'works' at the back, how they revolved the rear wheels and how the engine was started. One of the exhibition's oddest sights must have been that of the 'Steam Horse', the traction engine with the ordinary landau attached to its rear, lumbering around the enclosure with two rather brave ladies sitting in the landau.

Another demonstration showed climbing up an incline from flat ground. Then Salomons, deliberately flouting the law, drove his vehicle out of the show ground and along the public highway. This was to cock a snook at the laws in force against motor vehicles, the Locomotives & Highway Act, 1865, known as the 'Red Flag Act', which decreed all road vehicles thus propelled, at that time steam, should be attended by three people, one of whom was the man walking in front showing a red flag. Salomons, being a magistrate and the mayor, hoped to get away with this publicity – and he did.

At five o'clock the public went home, probably not realising they had seen a piece of automobile history, while organisers and exhibitors professed satisfaction with the day's results. The local *Kent and Sussex Courier* asked in its next edition: 'Will the horse of the future be fed upon petroleum instead of oats?'

Salomons was encouraged with four others to establish the British Motor Syndicate to develop motorisation in Britain. In 1896 he obtained the British manufacturing rights for the Voiturette, a two-seater one cylinder motor tricycle from Leon Bolle. Even more important, in 1896 Salomons got Parliament to repeal the law restricting the driving of motor vehicles. The victory was celebrated with a sightseeing demonstration on 15th November 1896, from London to Brighton, an event that still takes place annually. Salomons, unlike many pioneers, lived long enough to see the 'horseless carriage' he believed in developed as a common means of transport. He died in 1925 aged 74. The Tunbridge Wells Library Services' Showfields branch library has a plaque commemorating the first Horseless Carriage Exhibition.

Upchurch

Under the 14th century north chapel a medieval small crypt, charnel-house or 'bone hole' reached by a stairway and containing a collection of human bones, was discovered during a church restoration in 1877. This is not the same situation as the unsuspected chamber at St Nicholas-at-Wade, but follows that custom used at Hythe, although at the latter the skulls and bones have been stacked on shelves as a tourist attraction on payment of admission. When a churchyard became full, in order to make room for new burials after a sufficient period of time, the long dead were exhumed. Their bones were unceremoniously tipped into the 'bone hole' and covered. At Upchurch the bones were reinterred and the crypt sealed.

In the mid-16th century and later, numerous Acts of Parliament were passed to control creatures at the time considered 'vermin'. In Kent these Acts were administered by each parish vestry and they paid out sums from the parish rate to those who killed such creatures, various animals, birds, insects, even some species of caterpillars. At Upchurch in the 18th century the churchwarden's accounts recorded some of these payments: a fox's head was paid for with a shilling; a badger's head also at one shilling; a hedgehog for up to fourpence, sparrows at the rate of three shillings per dozen, while a polecat was rewarded with fourpence (see *Eastry, Borden*).

Upnor

On Ordnance Survey maps, on the Thames side of Yantlet Creek, about 8 miles north-east of Upnor, there is marked the 'London Stone', denoting that the river to this point is under the jurisdiction of the Lord Mayor of London and Port of London Authority. On the river front at Upnor there is another stone known as the London Stone, dated 1206, with the coat of arms and various inscription badly eroded and indecipherable. This Stone was formerly visited by London Lord Mayors who incised their now illegible names in it. This Stone's origin goes back to very old Charters and Acts that gave certain fishing rights to London fishermen in the Lower Medway. London's Lord Mayor was

The London Stone, Upnor

Conservator for the Thames and the Medway to this spot. Needless to say it caused much friction and fracas with the Medway fishermen. Near this Stone is another London Stone erected about 1836, marked with the names of London Lord Mayors and other City dignitaries.

Waldershare

➤ It is renowned for its park and Inigo Jones designed mansion, the exterior original, the interior a replica since a 1913 fire, but another interesting feature in one of the park's corners is an 18th century belvedere. A belvedere, like a gazebo (see *Northbourne* and *Faversham*) was a structure, this one being 60 ft high, a sort of useful folly from which the surrounding estate could be viewed in comfort. In a large double cube plan this belvedere was built with Portland stone between 1725-27 for Sir Robert Furnese, MP for New Romney. Sir Robert was the only son of Sir Henry Furnese from Sandwich, who made a fortune in London as a merchant and spent eight years from 1702 to 1710 planning and building the mansion and laying out the park. There is a first floor room with round-headed windows and smaller rooms above with rectangular windows, at the top being a balustrade. Sir Charles Igglesden, *A Saunter Through Kent*, Vol XX in 1927 said 'it is a dome-shaped building . . . and intended to be used as a music room. Its interior decorations were never completed, although portions of the work that remain show that the effect was to have been of an ornate character'. In 1907 another writer said that from its summit there was 'a magnificent view', a comment that would still apply. There are public footpaths in the park but the belvedere is not now accessible.

Waltham

➤ Over 50 years ago Sir Charles Igglesden, in his *A Saunter Through Kent*, Vol XXXII, wrote of this village: 'It stands in the centre of a plateau on the summit of the Downs. Waltham has no pretension to possessing a street specially picturesque. The Lord Nelson hostelry looks towards houses and cottages built apart and generally with bits of a garden, just an ordinary village street with no building boasting of great age'. That description fits today. Although some new houses and bungalows have infilled gaps at the road to Hastingleigh end of the village, at the Petham road end there is still an air of the properties just being plonked down, not in line, scattered hither and thither, without intention of formality. I think this casualness adds to any village's charm. Although it is not the highest point in Kent, that is claimed to be Betsoms Hill, Westerham, 811 ft above sea level, there is still, for me, a feeling of being high up on the roof of the Kentish Downs, accentuated by looking eastwards into the plunging valleys of tree and turf-covered slopes and farmed land.

Fixed to a fence by the lane leading to the church is an individual village sign, erected to commemorate the coronation of George VI and Queen Elizabeth. A white crown surmounts the words '12th May, 1937', below which is 'Waltham' in 'old English' lettering that any printer will recognise as Tudor Black type-face.

Down the wide Petham road, at the junction with the road to Anvil Green, stands Waltham Court, its sign declaring 'The Old Poor House 1796'. It had been started that year on the site, its construction completed in 1799 as a 'Poor House' (see *Westbere*), but it was closed in 1824 by which time being known as 'The Old Parish Work House'. A local miller, John Dilnot, bought it in 1826, making various changes. The refectory was used by the local Wesleyan Methodists as a Meeting House, the basement being divided into a bakehouse and, surprisingly, in view of the religious use above, a brewhouse, known as 'The Charity', run by a Julia Dilnot and Mrs Neame.

Services were held in the refectory until 1880 when the Wesleyan Methodists moved into their own new Meeting House closer to the village, closed in the 1960s and now converted into a private dwelling. In 1909 'The Old Parish Work House' had been bought by members of the Honywood family and also converted as a private residence called Waltham Court. After various successive owners, including army occupation in the 1939 War, it was converted postwar into an attractive hotel and restaurant. Thus do the fortunes of rural properties change for better or worse and in this case a former workhouse, in which labouring folk dreaded ending their days, is now a place in which people willingly pay to eat and be accommodated. Close by the old workhouse eight two-roomed cottages were built of which one survives, known as 'Court Cottage'.

Several signposts hereabouts point the way to a scattering of properties, Anvil Green, between the Petham road and Sole Street crossroads. The name may come from the Old English for Hagona's Open Land, corrupted with use to Hannafield by 1284, then to its present name. Sir Charles Igglesden, however, states that a local family named Handville lived here in a timber-framed house, with panels filled with herringbone-pattern brickwork. The type of residence and their name might suggest that as was commonplace at one time, the area took its name from this family. The house still exists and is called, according to its nameplate, Handville Green. Could this be an example where the lazy Kent speech, as evident in its dialect, was responsible for corrupting Handville into becoming Anvil? Perhaps, too, later generations eventually accepted the shorter version that sounded the same, for surveyors to more conveniently use on OS maps and fit on to signposts!

Westbere

It is downhill whichever of the three thoroughfares a visitor takes from the A28 Canterbury-Margate Roman road into Westbere's hidden village. While doing so there are panoramic views over Westbere Lakes, a wildlife sanctuary that evolved from former gravel extraction pits, showing that not all industrial penetration into the countryside need be for the worse. In Bushey Hill Road, the 14th century Yew Tree Inn with its adjoining yew, was a medieval hall house. It is reputed to be constructed with ships' timbers and this is not so unlikely when it is remembered the Westbere Levels here were formerly covered by an estuary and there was a wharf and relevant buildings. Excavations have discovered associated remains, iron ships' anchors and sundry items. Roman galleys sailed as far as hereabouts.

At the top and east side of Bushey Hill Road, on the south side of Island Road, was the Bread and Cheese Field, originally one acre, three rods, six perches in area. Prior to 1832 it was rented to one tenant to cultivate, but that year the lease expired and it was divided into portions as 'allotments for poor persons', at a low rent. The income from this source was used to pay for an annual Bread and Cheese Feast on Old Midsummer Day, 6th July, for all persons in the parish, the earliest existing record of this charity being churchwardens' accounts 1701 to 1784. The qualification to partake of it was that recipients must have slept in the parish three nights prior to the first Sunday after Old Midsummer Day. Each received bread and cheese and a pint of ale or strong beer, sometimes tobacco being supplied to men – and women. A record of it for 1834 states the Feast was held 'At the "Palm Tree" at 7.30 o'clock on Old Midsummer Day, 27 gallons of beer with bread and cheese was given away to 189 claimants'.

There was also a 'Bread and Cheese Cottage'. In 1794 a poorhouse was built on a corner of the Bread and Cheese Field, comprising four one-room tenements, two on the ground floor, two on the first floor, for relief of the Westbere poor, possibly four widows, one per room. Some of the field income was defrayed for the upkeep of the poorhouse accommodation. By 1834 it was known as 'Bread and Cheese Cottage' and a minimal rent levied, partly for upkeep of the property and a portion towards the Feast.

After 1884 beer was no longer given. In 1885 the field and cottage, which had formerly been managed separately, were combined, another change being that the income was also combined as a dole. Tickets for this were given to widows, others with more than two children too young to earn wages, elderly infirm and poor, in December, for bread and grocery. This amounted basically to a one shilling ticket for bread and a one shilling and sixpence ticket for grocery.

By 1961 the Bread and Cheese Cottage was in a condition needing much expenditure to bring it to 20th century standards, so the cottage and field were sold in 1962. The funds raised were invested but the Trustees, who had carried on their benevolence to worthy cases before and after the First and Second World Wars, continue today to make grants in kind and provide assistance to young people in their education and job training. On the cottage site properties have been built but its boundaries remain. The Bread and Cheese Field has no traces of the allotments and is now pasture.

The reference to the feast being held at the Palm Tree was not an error on the part of the earlier account writer. In a Kent custom, on Palm Sunday yew branches were used for house and church decoration as an alternative or if 'palm' (sallow, pussy-willow) was scarce. In Kent dialect yew was called 'palm' and the Yew Tree Inn thus was correctly known also as the Palm Tree Inn.

On the north side of the chancel of All Saints church is a memorial floor slab to twins, Thomas and Edmond Gilbert. Below the inscription is the likeness of two boys, standing holding hands. When faced, the boy on the left is to be seen holding the left hand of the other boy in his right hand, both clasped hands being approximately the centre of their abdomens, their other arms not being depicted. Their heads are not shown either. From their shoulders downwards the likenesses of the boys' torsos and legs and the lettering is deeply incised, but the black marble does not appear ever to have been incised where their heads should be. Nor does it seem to have been worn away. This may indicate the heads were never incised, nor their other arms, but why? They both lived about a year and died in 1640. Perhaps they were Siamese twins, joined at the head or shoulder. If they were they would have been considered 'monsters' at this period. To have depicted them correctly would have shown this noble family had created such offspring and so it was sort of hushed up.

Westerham

The vicinity of Westerham, on its greensand and chalk ridge, is terra firma now. However, almost 400 years ago, in 1596, an 'astonishing scene' occurred in this parish, about a mile and a half south of Westerham near the east side of a highway then called Ockham Hill. It will immediately be thought this should be Crockham Hill, but according to a map in Hasted's *History and Topographical Survey of Kent*, 1797, approximately this distance southeast from Westerham, between Crockham Hill (Hasted's name) and Horns Hill Common, stood Ockham House. So Ockham Hill appears a correct name for a hill in that area, as the account states. The earth, 'two closes separated by a hedge', sank over 80 ft.

According to Hasted 'This great trench of ground, containing in length 80 perches and in breadth 28 perches, began, with the hedges and trees thereon, to loose itself from the rest of the ground lying round about it and to slide and shoot altogether southward, day and night, for the space of 11 days.' Two water pits, one six ft deep, the other twelve ft deep, with alder and ash trees, were all 'removed out of their places and carried southward but also mounted aloft and became hills, with sedges, flags and black mud upon the tops of them, higher than the surface of the water they had forsaken. In the place from which they had moved other higher ground had descended and received the water on it'. In a field a hole 30 ft deep had sunk. A hedge with trees in it was also moved to the south and in other places in the area the earth had sunk so 'where the highest hills had been there were the deepest dales and where the lowest dales were before there was the highest ground'. Altogether over nine acres had been affected. The 'astonishing scene' had been witnessed by the local vicar, Sir John Studley, JP Robert Bostock and 'numerous others'.

Similarly, during spring 1756, at Toy's Hill, about a mile and a half east of where the above occurrence took place, on a two and a half acre field on the side of a hill facing south 'the land kept moving imperceptibly till the effect appeared, for some time, by which means the northern side was sunk two to three feet and became full of clefts and chasms, some only a foot deep, others as large as ponds, six or eight feet deep and ten to twelve feet square, most of them filled with water'. A hedge moved three rods to the south and from being straight was at an angle with its two ends. Another hedge 'separated to the distance of eight feet, the southern part of which was on a level before with the rest of the field, after this overhung it like a precipice, about the height of twelve feet; and the land on each side, which had not moved, was covered with the rest, which folded over it, to the height of six or seven feet'. What was the cause of these 'astonishing scenes'? Landslips seem probable. A collapse of underground strata? A minor earthquake on both occasions? The latter is not so unlikely (see *Edenbridge*). Whatever it was the earth certainly moved for the local inhabitants of the area in 1596 and 1756.

West Kingsdown

West Kingsdown's black weatherboarded smock windmill, with white sweeps and fantail, near the A20, started life elsewhere, having been moved several miles south-east from Farningham in 1880. Although it would seem unlikely, windmills, particularly post mills, were quite frequently moved to different sites, sometimes in search of better wind conditions. If not too far away the sweeps, stones and transmission gear were removed, the windmill jacked up, put on to a horse-drawn six-wheeled trolley and, still vertical, trundled to the new site. In another instance, a Petham miller moved to Stelling Minnis in 1840 and took his windmill with him, requiring, it has been estimated, seven pairs of Shire horses to haul it up some of the hills (see *Wittersham*).

A mile and a quarter west of St Edmund's church, which is hidden in a wood, is another Kent ruined church, the Early Norman Maplescombe church. All that survives of the nave and chancel is a length of flint wall.

In 1851 a Major Vincent, a surgeon at Guy's Hospital, London, paid for a new church to be built at the southern end of Knatt's Valley as part of a new residential parish called Woodlands, a school and vicarage, all with bell-gables, also being built, the school in the same shape as the church. The area still has a remoteness about it which is probably what attracted the Major to the area to 'get away from it all' (see *Lower Hardres*).

West Peckham

➤ On a hill above the village is the site of Diamond's Cottage. Jack Diamond lived there and was supposedly a highwayman. The cottage is said to have mysteriously burnt down on a Friday the 13th. It is also reputed Diamond's ghost appears there on that date and this was so on Friday 13th May 1961.

West Wickham

➤ In the early 19th century during Rogation week an ancient custom called 'youling' used to take place in the Wickham area. In this a group of young men would run into apple orchards and in turn encircle each tree. While doing this as noisily as possible they would utter words: 'Stand fast root, Bear well top, God send us a youling crop, Every twig apple big, Every bough apple enow'.

Rogation week is the week in which 'Rogation days' fall. The 'Rogation days' are the three days before Ascension Day, on which the litany is, or was, sung in procession, often with special petitions for a blessing on the crops. In some areas, one being Newington-by-Sittingbourne, it was the custom to bless the cherry blossom in local orchards, the vicar, choir and congregation processing from the church.

No doubt 'youling' was based on pagan practices and has similarities to the West Country 'wassailing' custom that takes place earlier in the year, except in the latter participants are well fortified with cider, which is also splashed on the trees during the recitations in the orchards.

I have been told that the first supermarket in Kent was built at West Wickham in the 1960s as an experimental tryout. Now look how many there are!

Whitstable

➤ Sheerness has its folly 'ship on shore' and an inn alongside it thus named, but Whitstable has the real thing. Between the sea-wall and Island Wall, near Waterloo Road, a gap among some cottages is the final berth of the *Favourite*, a Whitstable oyster yawl. She was built locally in 1890 by the Whitstable Shipping Company some 30 yards away from her present situation, for the proprietors

Another 'ship on shore', Whitstable's oyster yawl *Favourite*

of the Fisherman's Arms. Shipyard Cottages was at that time a forge and herein the iron parts were made for the *Favourite*. Her dimensions are length 39 ft 3 inches; beam twelve ft three inches, height of hold five ft, displacement 16.8 tons, requiring a crew of up to three men and a boy. The shallow draught allowed for use in local shoal waters. Her first owners used her mainly for oyster dredging. In 1918 the Whitstable Oyster Fishing Company bought and worked her for 20 years, but gradually less so as she was not motorised.

In 1940 she was hauled up on a Whitstable slipway and while there machine gunned by an enemy seaplane. Until 1952 she lay unused on the beach then the Whistable Oyster Fishing Company sold her for £100. She was beyond restoration by her new owner but when plans were introduced to build an improved sea-wall to protect the cottages against flooding along this area he decided to have her hauled off the beach and finally into this gap. The full details of how this was achieved are told by P.J. Banbury in *Whitstable Oyster Yawl 'Favourite' 1890-1980* (*Bygone Kent*, February, 1980). She remains where she was hauled to this day, maintained as well as can be but she ought to be under cover. However at least this hard-working vessel at the end of her career has not suffered the ignominious fate of being hulked somewhere on the Medway mudflats or burnt on the beach.

Still to be seen from the Keam's Yard section of the new sea-wall looking west is a long brick building. This belonged to Thomas Gann and Co, boatbuilders founded in 1846. Here in July 1876 was constructed the largest ship built in Whitstable, the *Nellie S*, a brigantine, 131 ft long, beam 26 ft, 282 reg. tons. Her owner was George Henry Gann who kept her for the firm's use in the South American trade, especially carrying railway track there and returning

183

with mahogany from Mexico. Wallace Harvey in his *The Merchant Ships of Whitstable* (Emprint Publishers, 1993) states she was built of English oak and African hardwood obtained from ships broken up in Chatham Dockyard. She was sold in 1883 and went to a Cornish owner.

I discovered a strange coincidence with another of the Gann built ships. On 15th January 1861, the *Fanny Gann*, a 97 ton schooner built at Whitstable in 1850 owned by Thomas Gann, Snr, its builder, was sailing off Folkestone when she was struck by a German brig from Bremen. This occurred with some force so the *Fanny Gann's* masts were carried overboard. At the time the ship's boy named Greenland was aloft reefing and he was flung with the masts and rigging into the sea and drowned. The rest of the crew and captain got aboard the German brig that towed the disabled *Fanny Gann* into Ramsgate. The sad result of the accident was that the lad's parents offered a reward of £2 for the recovery of his body. The amazing coincidence is that in Lydd churchyard is the empty grave with a memorial stone to another ship's lad with this surname, Edward Greenland, aged 17, who also fell from his ship's rigging off Yokohama and was drowned, though nine years later, in 1870 (see *Lydd*).

Near to the Keam's Yard section is a wood plaque on the wall reading 'Cushing's View', placed there to honour Peter Cushing, the film actor, a resident of Whitstable for many years and often to be seen on this part of the local shore.

Further east, past Horsebridge and closer to the Harbour, is Reeve's Beach and a section of sea defences wall completed in 1989. The beach here got its name from William Reeves of the Company of Oyster Fishers. In 1794 he enclosed some waste ground on the waterfront and developed a family business of timber merchants, block and mast making. In 1869, owned by descendants Elizabeth and Josiah Reeves, along with other trade developments on the front it was devastated by a fire that swept through the area's stores, workshops and yards. In 1900 a George Warner bought the seaward side of the site, the landward side up to Sea Street in 1902, for use as a marine dealer's yard. In 1913 it was proposed Whitstable Urban District Council buy the now derelict site and after some objections from rate-payers a company was founded, the site laid out as a concrete or stone floor skating rink and with a Tudor Tea Rooms built at the eastern end. Part of the rink was in the open, the other covered with a large span roof incorporating an unusual, now rare, method of roof construction. This long building is still part of the site with corrugated iron sides and a curved corrugated iron roof, though the old rusting exterior does not indicate how interesting this building is. The corrugated iron roof is supported by a series of girders and scissor-like cross-pieces known as the 'Belfast Truss' method. It was decided by the council to call the site 'The Rink', but the local users, due to its shape, called it 'The Oval'. Eventually the craze for roller skating passed and in 1944 Whitstable Urban District Council, instead of leasing as they had from 1913, decided to buy the site for £300. Today the open area is a parking lot for marine craft, the corrugated iron building used as a do-it-yourself retail shop.

It is stated in guide books that nothing is surviving of the actual 'Crab and Winkle' railway line that linked Whitstable Harbour to Canterbury. This is not so. In Harbour Street, opposite Gorrells Tank, for example, there are two large wrought iron gates that allow access to the Harbour and on them are the original four London, Chatham and Dover Railway badges, one on each side of each gate.

Wickhambreaux

➤Americans make a point of visiting St Andrew's church to see the east window and its American stained glass that, according to the *New York Times* in 1896, was the first commission from Europe given to American glassworkers. The Art Nouveaux glass is a unique representation of the Annunciation, dated 1896, signed Arild Rosenkrantz. It was given to the church in memory of the Countess de Gallatin by her only son, she being interred in the churchyard. The Tudor Old Bellhouse nearby, originally the Bellhouse, is so named possibly because in 1525 on his decease the owner decreed the sum raised from renting it to a tenant should be used to pay for the ringing of the curfew bell. When Nonconformism was increasing in the area a room was used in the Bellhouse as a school for the teaching of the children of Nonconformist parents who had been refused admission for education at the Church of England school.

Wittersham

➤The Stocks windmill, a post mill (see *West Kingsdown*) is a complete contrast, weatherboarded white and brick base black painted, being kept in fine condition by a local committee. The centre post has the date 1781. In the hamlet of The Stocks one of the properties has a façade of fish-scale tiles.

James Antony Syms in his *Kent Country Churches Continued* writes of St John's church 'The tower is topped by an elegant vane, dated 1751, which I have read, makes it almost the oldest dated vane in Kent' (see *Stockbury*).

Wye

On the North Downs near Wye, above an old chalk pit, there is a crown cut in the turf. Visible from afar today, in the recent past it was deliberately hidden for national security reasons.

The crown is 180 ft wide at its base, approximately 180 ft high, with a trench about 13 ft wide outlining it. It had been suggested by the principal of the nearby Wye College at the time to mark the coronation of Edward VII. Gangs of college students did the digging to expose the chalk and create the crown, the chalk spoil removed being wheelbarrowed into the convenient chalk pit. An ingenious idea was used to allow it to be cut accurately. A paper shape of a crown, similar to the shape of the crown on the old silver double florin, was stuck on the object lens of a theodolite. Then students using flags on poles were directed into position around the outline of the crown on the Downland slope with hand signals until it was correct in shape from a distance. This plan was then triangulated and laid down to a scale on paper. Fifteen hundred fairy lamps were used to illuminate the shape of the crown on Coronation Night 1902. It was also lit on George Vs Silver Jubilee in 1935 and Elizabeth II's Jubilee in 1977.

At the outbreak of the Second World War it was realised its visible shape could be used by enemy aircraft navigators to plot their course. So for almost five years the crown was hidden under a covering of brushwood believed to have been applied by a military camouflage expert as it was so skilfully done. It was last 'scoured' to restore its white outline on the 80th anniversary of its original creation, in June 1982.

Yalding

There is a common expression 'a skeleton in the cupboard', in reference to someone or a family who has something to hide, the secret of which is carefully guarded. It may sound like a rural yarn but at the 17th century Woolpack Inn, Benover, Yalding, there *is* a skeleton in a cupboard. It will be revealed by the landlord on customers' request. It used to be seated at the corner of the counter in one of the bars, but it tended to alarm some of the customers. So a previous landlord 'imprisoned' the skeleton in a cupboard under some stairs, with an iron grid over a glass panel in the door to allow it to be viewed.

There is another instance concerning Yalding that also may sound like a fisherman's yarn. In 1757 a large eel was caught in the river Medway hereabouts. It measured five ft nine inches long, 18 inches in girth and weighed over 40 pounds. Bagshaw's 1847 *County Gazetteer* records the catch.

Yalding had another record – regarding hops. The soil being very productive, 5,813 acres of land in a parish six miles by four miles was under cultivation, 1,100 of these being hop gardens growing hops. In the 1920s this was the largest hop growing parish in Kent and therefore possibly in England.

Bibliography

ALLINSON, Helen, *Borden – The History of a Kentish Parish* Synjon Books, 1992

BALDWIN, Michael *The River and the Downs* Gollancz 1984

BANBURY, P.J. *Whitstable Oyster Yawl 'Favourite', 1890-1980* Bygone Kent, February 1980

CAMPBELL, Donald *A Short Guide to St Peter and St Paul Church, Farningham* 1973

CHOWNS, L.M. *Shadoxhurst – A Village History* Privately published 1977

DAVEY, G. *A Guide to St Mary's*, Chiddingstone Parish Church Council

FIELDING, C.H. *Memories of Malling and its Valley* Henry Oliver 1893

FILMER, Richard *Old Ashford* Alan Sutton 1988

GERRISH, Pat *David Salomons House, Southborough*

GOODSALL, Robert *The Medway and its Tributaries* Constable 1955

GOWERS, Edward and CHURCH, Derek *Across the Low Meadow* Christine Swift 1979

HARVEY, Wallace *The Merchant Ships of Whitstable* Emprint Publishers 1993

JONES, John B. *Dover* 1907

JUDGE, Sheila *The Isle of Sheppey* Rochester Press 1983

LAPTHORNE, W.H. *A Broad Place* Privately published, available locally

LAPTHORNE, W.H. *Historic Broadstairs* Privately published, available locally

MACDOUGALL, P. *The Hoo Peninsula* John Hallewell 1980

McINTOSH, K.H. *Chislet and Westbere* Published by the author

McINTOSH, K.H. *Sturry,the Changing Scene* Published by the author

MAJOR, Alan Various articles published in *Bygone Kent* Meresborough Books

NEWMAN, John *West Kent and the Weald* Penguin Books 1969

NEWMAN, Paul *Gods and Graven Images* Robert Hale

RITCHIE, C.I.A. *Dartford's Doubtful Eldorado* 'Kent Life' October 1964

ROPER, Anne *The Gift of the Sea – Romney Marsh* Birlings 1984

ROPER, Anne *The Church of St Clement* Old Romney Church Guide

SMITH, W.J. *The History of Rainham* Privately published 1937
SPELLING, R.S. *Tenterden* Locally published
SYMS, James A. *Kent Country Churches Continued* Meresborough
    Books 1987
TAPSELL, Martin *Memories of Kent Cinemas* Plateway Press
THOMPSON, J.R.V. *The House on the Hill – a Petham Record*
    Published privately 1988
WILLIAMS, I. *A Short History of Elham and its Parish Church*
    1959

Coal Posts in Bromley Environment Bromley booklet
Hollingbourne Memorial booklet to Ethel de Visine Thomas,
    Eyhorne House 1963
Ightham Church Guide 1975
Patrixbourne, *St Mary's Church Guide*
Tenterden, *The Parish Church of St Mildred Guide*
Wickhambreaux Guide, published by the Ickham, Wingham and
    District Residents Association

Index